ALTRUISM

ITS NATURE AND VARIETIES

ALTRUISM

ITS NATURE AND VARIETIES

THE ELY LECTURES FOR 1917–18

BY

GEORGE HERBERT PALMER

CHARLES SCRIBNER'S SONS
NEW YORK 〟 〟 〟 〟 1919

THE ELY FOUNDATION

The Elias P. Ely Lectureship was founded by Mr. Zebulon Stiles Ely, May 8, 1865. The deed of gift contains the following paragraphs:

"The undersigned gives the sum of ten thousand dollars to the Union Theological Seminary of the City of New York to found a Lectureship in the same, the title of which shall be the 'Elias P. Ely Lectures on the Evidences of Christianity,' on the following conditions:

"The course of lectures given on this foundation is to comprise any topics that serve to establish the proposition that Christianity is a religion from God, or that it is the perfect and final form of religion for man. Among the subjects discussed may be the nature and need of a revelation; the character and influence of Christ and His apostles; the authenticity and credibility of the Scriptures, miracles, and prophecy; the diffusion and benefits of Christianity; the philosophy of religion in its relation to the Christian system."

Under date of May 24, 1879, Mr. Ely addressed a communication to the Directors of the Seminary in which the conditions of the Lectureship are amplified as follows:

"The conditions of the foundation of the Elias P. Ely Lectureship, dated May 8, 1865, are hereby modified, so that the course of public lectures therein provided for, may not only be on 'The Evidences of Christianity,' but on such other subjects as the Faculty and Directors, in concurrence with the undersigned, while living, may deem for the good of man."

PREFACE

I here present the substance of eight Ely Lectures delivered in the spring of 1918 at Union Theological Seminary in New York. They were spoken without manuscript. In writing them out from the stenographer's notes I have condensed them considerably. In these belligerent days publishers are disposed to economize paper and print, and readers to prize brevity in everything except newspapers. Such restrictions force on us loquacious book-makers greater regard for compactness and lucidity, and are thus not altogether an injury.

The book seeks to call attention to a section of ethics in regard to which the public mind greatly needs clarifying. Altruism and egoism, socialism and individualism, are in our time sentimentally arrayed against one another as independent and antagonistic agencies, each having its partisans. A careful examination will show,

I think, that the one has meaning only when in company with its supposed rival. I have thought to make this clearest by tracing three stages through which the altruistic impulse passes in every-day life, exhibiting their varying degrees of dignity and the helpful presence in all of them of egoistic balance. If through my notion of a conjunct self I have made this curious partnership plain I shall count it no mean contribution to our generous, sacrificial, self-assertive, and perplexed time.

GEORGE HERBERT PALMER.

CAMBRIDGE, October 21, 1918.

CONTENTS

ALTRUISM
ITS NATURE AND VARIETIES

CHAPTER I

INTRODUCTION

I HAVE been moving about lately through different parts of our country, sitting down to dinner in many homes, and I have everywhere found the family eating bread made of Indian meal, rye, barley, or oatmeal. When I have asked, "Are you especially fond of this sort of food?" I have pretty generally received the answer, "Why, no! We all like wheat bread better. But we are not eating it now, for other nations need it."

That is altruism, one of the most fundamental, familiar, and mysterious of all the virtues. This course of lectures will be devoted to elucidating it. To a recognition of it the Western mind has risen slowly. The Greeks attached little importance to it; for though philanthropy, regard for

man as man, is a Greek word, it is not a
Greek idea. Plato does not include it
among his four virtues nor anywhere lay
stress on its practice. In Aristotle's *Ethics*,
it is true, there are magnificent chapters
on friendship, and friendship plays a great
part in the teaching of the Epicureans and
Stoics. But all alike speak of attachment
to another person chiefly as a means of
strength for oneself. The thought of
whole-hearted giving without correspondent
personal gain would have puzzled a Greek.

When we turn to the other branch of
our civilization and examine what we have
derived from the Hebrews, we find a
nearer approach to modern ideas. Commonly enough the Hebrews speak of mercy
and grace, and pair these off against justice and truth. Apparently when these
terms are applied to God's dealings with
us, the second pair indicates his exact return for what we have done for him; but
the first pair points to something over and
above, a surplusage of generosity, lying
outside the field of equal pay. God is conceived as altruistic and we are summoned
to imitate him in this. Jesus develops the
thought to such a degree that love be-

comes the centre of his teaching. We are told that without it all other excellence is worthless. We must love as God loves, letting our sun shine on the evil and on the good. Indeed, we must love even our enemies.

While modern nations have allowed such precepts to stand as counsels of perfection and have been ready to see in occasional acts an embodiment of them, parallel with them they have always recognized a contrary and more powerful tendency, namely, the disposition to seek one's own. This they have believed to be essential for carrying on the daily affairs of life. At the same time altruistic conduct has ever been thought "superior," "higher"; egoistic, as containing nothing to call forth admiration.

When men, however, began to think seriously about ethics it became impossible to allow two such springs of action to remain in permanent discord. Attempts were made to bring them into harmony by showing that the one is only a disguised form of the other. Hobbes, for example (1588–1679), the first in his great book, *Leviathan*, to stir the English mind to ethical reflection, maintains that altruism is strictly impossible. Each of us seeks self-preservation and acts through a passion for power. This necessarily brings us into conflict with our neighbors and makes of society a strife of each with all. Such universal war is soon seen to bring damage to every one and social compacts arise, compromises, under which I concede to others the right of acting in certain ways on condition of their allowing my action in certain others. While this involves large sacrifice of one's own desires for the sake of other people, it is endured because it pays, pays egoistically. We gain by it the largest scope for action our crowded world permits. But there is nothing disinterested about it. Genuine altruism is nowhere operative. A man cannot escape from himself and feel another's pleasure as his own. As well might I profess to feel your toothache more keenly than my own as to declare myself more interested in your welfare than in that of myself. Fundamentally, each of us must be egoistic; but we can be successfully so only by taking others into the account.

This attempt of Hobbes to resolve altruism into a larger form of egoism naturally

shocked England, and a century was spent
by the English moralists in trying to prove
that the benevolent feelings are equally
original with the self-seeking. Cumber-
land, Shaftesbury, Hutcheson, Butler, eagerly demonstrated benevolence to be a
constant and independent factor of human
life; but when they attempted to show the
relation in which this stands to its seeming
opposite, they became vague. Apparently
there are two rival forces within us. Now
one acts, now the other.

A few of the attempts that have been
made to effect a junction of the two, and to
show how we cross from our egoistic to
altruistic desires, deserve notice. Hartley
(1705–1757) proposed an ingenious one.
The two passions become fused through
association. We are all familiar with the
man who begins to accumulate money in
order to supply his daily wants and then
by degrees withdraws his attention from
those wants and fixes it upon money itself.
What was originally a means becomes an
end. In just this way Hartley thought our
egoistic desires become transformed. To
reach satisfaction they usually require as-
sistance from other people. Conscious at

first of our dependence on others for aid,
we become by degrees interested in others
for their own sake, and finally seek to aid
them rather than have them aid us. Our
self-regarding powers and our extra-re-
garding powers are thus by association
blurred into one. An important school of
ethical writers, among whom the two Mills
are the most notable, have held this view.

An interesting variation was adopted by
Jeremy Bentham (1748–1832). It might
be called the quantitative view. The one
thing desired by us all is happiness. We
seek to produce as much of it as possible,
paying little attention to the one on whom
it falls. Of course our primary desire looks
toward ourselves. But in seeking to increase that bulk of happiness from which
we draw, egoism largely disappears in the
search after the greatest happiness of the
greatest number. This formula must always be convenient and valuable in a
democratic state.

One of the most curious of these methods of extracting altruistic gold from a
baser metal is that of Bishop Paley (1743–
1805). According to him we have none of
us an interest in our fellows' happiness and

should never of ourselves seek it. But we read in our Bibles the command to love our neighbor and are told that we shall fall into eternal misery if we do not. With his customary audacious clearness Paley states the matter thus: "The greatest virtue is doing good to mankind, in obedience to the will of God, and for the sake of everlasting happiness." That is, the one thing of importance is altruistic endeavor. But this is so alien to our disposition that it can be brought about only through divine interposition, making it a condition of our own permanent enjoyment.

A subtler doctrine, and one much closer to the facts of human nature, is that of Adam Smith (1723–1790). He has observed how large a part sympathy plays in our ordinary affairs. If I am near a person when he is moved by any feeling, that feeling tends to jump across and to become mine also. Such identification of myself and him gives pleasure to us both. We all have experienced how sympathy heightens enjoyment and diminishes distress. In sympathy two sets of feelings become so nearly identified that the result can be called neither egoistic nor altruistic.

Now I do not propose in these lectures
to combat or defend any of these theories.
No one of them seems to me to be without
weight, all deserve consideration, and something like the operation of each I trace in
people around me. The one with which I
am in largest agreement is the last, where
Adam Smith would identify the two moral
aims. But all the theories are vitiated by
a false start, which in these lectures I wish
to avoid.

Each of them looks upon man in his
original estate as a self-centred being, a
distinct ego. By degrees this single person
discovers other persons about him and
learns that he must have relations with
them. The relations may be altruistic or
egoistic, but they are subsequent and supplemental. In himself he is separate and
detached. Now, I hold that this conception is altogether erroneous. There is no
such solitary person. One person is no
person. The smallest known unit of personality is three, father, mother, child.
None of us came into the world in sepa-
rateness, nor have separately remained here.
Relations have encompassed us from birth.
Through them we are what we are, social

beings, members of a whole. While it is true that the ties of parentage loosen as the child matures, these drop away only because others, now more formative, take him in charge. Before we have a separate consciousness we know ourselves as members of a family, of a state, of the community of human kind. We never stand alone.

Not that it is an error to say "I." This, properly, is our commonest word and commonest thought. Only with reference to it does anything else have value. However interlocked the total frame of things may be, at certain centres where relations converge there are unique spots of consciousness capable of estimating reality and of sending forth modifying influences. Such a centre of consciousness, unlike all else, we rightly call a person, a self or ego; and because of its importance we often fix attention on it, withdrawing notice for the moment from the relations which encompass it. Such an abstraction, if clearly understood, is entirely legitimate. I shall frequently make use of it under the title of the separate or abstract self. But it should be borne in mind that it is an ab-

straction and that the real person is what
I shall call the conjunct or social self, made
up of that centre of consciousness and the
relations in which it stands. While these
two are usefully distinguishable, they are
not separable. When I try to detach myself from my surroundings I know I am
attempting an impossibility. How much
would there be left of me were there no one
but this central ego, none with whom I
might communicate, no language prepared
for communication or thought, no common
affections, interests, or undertakings? Evidently we are from the start social beings.
If with the early moralists we make the
opposite assumption, our subsequent interest in our fellow men will never quite clear
itself of artificiality and mistake.

Yet while the separate self and the conjunct self lodge in the same being, the degree and kind of attention accorded to the
latter marks the stage of moral maturity
at which man or nation has arrived. In
certain undeveloped forms of social life the
conjunctive elements are but slightly emphasized, while the separate self bulks
large. With the advance of morality the
opposite principle obtains. Wider and

more subtle relationships are seen to make
our lives our own. Many as are these
social varieties, I have thought they might
advantageously be examined under three
headings, to which I give the rather unin-
telligible names of Manners, Gifts, and
Mutuality. While recognizing that every
phase of human life is altruistic in some
degree, I hold that there are higher grades
which give to the principle a prominence
and scope which the lower lack. My general subject, then, might be entitled The
Forms and Stages of the Conjunct Self.
I begin where the conjunctive principle appears in its narrowest range and advance
into the broader altruism only as I am
logically compelled to do so. Endeavor-
ing to see how small a section of human
conduct need be affected by altruism, I am
ultimately forced to make it as extensive as
life itself.

Maintaining, however, as I do, that the
two contrasted elements always are and
should be mutually serviceable, I naturally have nothing to say in condemnation
of self-seeking. On the contrary, I hold it
to be praiseworthy. Rightly does Aristotle assert that the good man is always a

lover of himself. But of which self is Aristotle thinking, the conjunct or the separate? Much of the mystery surrounding the notion of altruism is due to confusion on this point. For example, when a man is charged with selfishness it is usually because he is thought to have obtained some advantage. But why should he not? He is blamable only when he detaches the thought of his own advantage from advantage to others. My good must not be had at another's expense. When a plate of apples is passed and I pick out the best one, the wrong is not in my obtaining a good apple but in my depriving somebody else of one. That is selfishness. Whenever my gain is not inconsistent with his or, as is usually the case, actually contributes to it, the larger the gain made by me the better.

CHAPTER II

MANNERS

WHERE, then, does altruism appear in its simplest form? Whenever one of us comes into the presence of another there occurs a subtle change of personal attitude to which I give the name of Manners. We do not act or speak precisely as if alone. In all our bearing there is a marked adjustment of one personality to another. I take on the color of him before whom I stand. I feel his psychological conditions and square myself accordingly. That is, I at once perceive that he and I are not quite independent. An acknowledgment of a certain community between us must be established before either of us can be at ease. Such acknowledgment may have a wide or narrow scope, but it will always imply regard for another for his own sake and not merely regard for my sake.

One would expect that the words which name a relation so normal and dignified would be words suggestive of honor.

Strangely enough, they are all depreciatory. I have sought for a word to describe the consideration of man by man which would be colorless, that neither praised nor blamed, but simply fixed attention on the fact. No such word do I find. A blot of disparagement is on them all. I choose Manners as on the whole the least objectionable.

Pass them briefly in review. When I say a man is kind in Manners, do I not suggest that there may be a contrast between his outward bearing and his inner heart? Or shall we call the relation one of Propriety, as Adam Smith does in his masterly discussion of this moral situation? Propriety always stirs aversion, because it implies that we have had little share in establishing the standard employed. It has been set up outside us and still we are subjected to it. How exasperated a child is when told to behave properly! Why should he care for Propriety? Or shall we say Civility? It is a scrimping, meagre word, announcing that only so much consideration is shown as decency requires. When we hear a man say, "John was civil to me," our thought continues: "Was that

all? Did he go no further than that?"
How would Politeness do? More than
Manners it hints at insincerity and conduct that hopes to gain something for itself. Beware of a polite man. He is
likely to use you for his own ends. Might
we then talk of Good Breeding? When
any one calls me well-bred he praises my
parents, not me. The excellence on which
I pride myself has apparently come from
their training. What shall we say of Courtesy? That it is a term of dignity, but
suggests stooping. The one with whom I
deal is accounted my inferior. Or Gentle-
manliness? To call a young fellow a gentleman makes his heart throb. Yet the
word does not escape a certain limitation.
It uses the standard of a particular set,
"our crowd." If my conduct does not accord with their usages, I am not a gentleman. The word lacks universality.

By such questionable terms our language
names the beautiful relation I am now to
set forth. Since Manners is on the whole
the least stained word among them, the
one most nearly neutral, I adopt it, but I
shall read into it much more meaning than
people generally intend. To cover its

full meaning I am obliged to frame a
statement so burdened with details that
it will hardly be recognized as anything
commonly called Manners. But it shall be
explained clause by clause, and I ask my
reader to watch whether I have introduced
anything into it which might be omitted or
omitted anything which should have been
introduced. The definition runs thus: By
Manners I mean such a voluntary conformity to a code of conduct as, within a
fixed field of intercourse, insures to each
person the least offense and a due opportunity of self-expression. Four elements
are here named as belonging to Manners.
I will take them up separately and in order.

In the first place Manners assume a settled code, a social arrangement generally
agreed to. They are essentially systematic, not impulsive and incidental. An ex-
clamation of joy uttered when I am happy
may or may not be consistent with good
manners. That depends on how fully it
has been rationalized. I am expected to
act to-day as I should wish to act to-
morrow. Expression must keep in view
the whole personality. Moreover, I must
know how other people act and bring my

action into measurable conformity with theirs. If I am frequently doing what nobody else does, I am sure to be thought rude. I am expected to understand what the social code demands. Perhaps the word "code" is too formal. It pictures a committee drawing up a plan of behavior. Of course no such committee exists. Yet an agreement there has been, a tacit understanding, of how we are to behave to one another. Any one ignorant of this understanding, or neglectful of it, is reckoned boorish and unfit for mannerly intercourse. That usage and not my own liking should direct my bearing toward others. To do something just because I like to shows me uncivilized. My commonest actions should be socialized. They are expected to express something more than my separate self, namely, my conjunct self, showing accordance with myself at other times and also accordance with the persons around me.

Is it well or usual to have these understandings written down? Are manuals of manners useful, teaching us just how to behave in this and that situation? Such books exist, but I believe few would will-

ingly be caught reading one. Formal
codes are not what we want. They are
not fine enough. They study moral situations too mechanically, with too little regard for personality. From them one
might pick up a few useful warnings about
certain bad habits not previously noticed;
but a man who followed such a manual ex-
actly would nowhere be a welcome guest.

Conformity to a standard, however, is
far from the whole of manners. Were it
so, the place to find good manners would
be the State Prison. A clear code is established there. Each man is told precisely what he is to do throughout the entire day. For that reason we are hardly
justified in speaking of convict manners at
all. A prison permits no expression of the
individual life, and a second condition of
good manners was "*voluntary* conformity
to a social code." While every child should
be trained to know how those who are
wisest and kindest are accustomed to meet
the little circumstances of daily intercourse, still that child's actions are worthless if they do not bear his own stamp. Is
not this what we mean by a vulgar man?
His manners are not an expression of him-

self, but of somebody else. Other men have
obliterated him. An evident copy is all
that remains. Fine manners play around
the correct modes, departing from them
here and there in little niceties. So far is
the code from fettering individuality that it
becomes the channel for its easiest outgo.
A graceful gentleman is enviable in his
freedom. He is at home anywhere. Every
situation has been thought out by society
beforehand. With its conclusions he has
been long acquainted and in his own way
swiftly adapts them to the delicate occasion at hand. There is no surprise, no
awkwardness, no loss of dignity. The
separate self is not altogether suppressed,
but is present everywhere in the service of
the conjunct.

There appears in the definition, however,
a phrase which clogs it: "Within a fixed
field of intercourse." Why is this necessary and what does it mean? Manners
need to be adjusted to different occasions.
Those that are suitable to the shop do not
fit the evening party. When we meet for
the exchange of commodities or meet to
exchange good wishes and general good
cheer, we approach one another from dif-

ferent angles, and our manners should reflect them appropriately. When again we meet for discussion, the social situation is so peculiar that nothing less than a written code, a *Cushing's Manual*, will insure freedom for all. Left to themselves, each person would speak as often as feeling prompted. But such rude manners are not allowed. No one must speak without appealing to the chairman and receiving his permission by word or nod. If a person opposing me in debate makes statements which strike me as absurd and intended to mislead, I am not at liberty to characterize them so. Debate could not proceed on such terms. Every one must be respectful and conform to a parliamentary standard. Such a standard would be out of place in the home. But much of the beauty of human intercourse arises from noticing these differences in the field and, with full knowledge of what is customary, adapting our manners freshly to what the occasions require.

But readers will already be asking, "Why all this pomp and circumstance? What object can make us willing to accept such constraint instead of approaching one an-

other as we happen to feel." That object
was the fourth point in my definition:
Manners are accepted "in order to insure
to each person the least offense and a due
opportunity for self-expression." Expression is dear to all. At least to me it is always a pleasure to give another a piece of
my mind. This may not be a pleasure to
that other. If, then, we are to be social
beings, there must be some security that
when I am enjoying speech I cause no disturbance to others. Accordingly, the chief
object of manners is a negative one, to
avoid offense, to put every one at ease.
Suppose the contrary; suppose A. B. asks
me to meet a group of his friends; suppose
I have a fancy for colored waistcoats and
dress of fantastic design; suppose me not
inclined to subordinate my taste to that of
others, but simply to dress as I please.
Should I not come as an intruder and disturber, preventing my fellow guests from
thinking of anything but me? I should
not be invited again to that house. To
avoid such scenes we willingly accept a
common costume, which nobody was ever
known to admire. We go out in the evening garbed in black. We know then what

to expect, securing ourselves against shock and curbing the self-asserter. That turbulent ego is the chief obstacle to society. Better give up much that is of value if we can thus be brought to conduct which shows consideration for all around.

The other part of the aim of manners, self-expression, is subordinate though desirable. Living alone, we are small; in contact with our fellow men, we enlarge ourselves. Trouble is worth taking for such a purpose. But there are dangers. Society is possible only where mutual consideration is shown. To be a social person one must be altruistically minded, continually studying another's comfort. I am talking with two or three old friends about some experiences of our youth, when John Smith joins us. We go on talking, and soon all the company except John Smith bursts into laughter. He naturally feels shut out and we perceive that we have been rude. Manners are devised to stop such painful feelings. We leave outside social walls whatever cannot be shared by all alike.

I have been expounding here something so familiar that it is seldom mentioned or even thought of, but is usually taken as a matter of course. Yet surely it is important to perceive how wide is the extent of altruism. It is nothing occasional, calling for exceptional heroism. It is commonplace, spread all around us, attending the most elementary processes of existence. We never approach one another as separate beings, but are called on wherever we meet to put each other at ease, whatever may be the cost to ourselves. Well does Bentham write: "Good breeding is that deportment on occasions of inferior, and, when separately taken, of trivial importance by which those acts are abstained from which give annoyance to others. It is to this negative or abstinential branch of benevolence that most of the laws of good breeding are to be referred." Christ in offering the Golden Rule seems not to be urging unusual conduct, but rather to suggest that we carry out consistently and as a plan of life a principle inwrought into the very structure of our being. We are made conjunctive. Any attempt to exhibit the varieties of altruism must take this beautiful fact as its starting-point.

No one has set forth more clearly the

scope and delicacy of manners than Adam
Smith in those chapters of his *Moral Senti-
ments* which treat of Propriety. He asks
what feelings may properly be expressed in
company and what others, equally natural,
the well-mannered man suppresses. The
general principle is that those which have
their root in specific circumstances of the
individual, as, for example, the physical
experiences, should be kept in the background. A gentleman does not talk of his
toothache or recent cold, nor does he show
his strong appetite at table. While recognizing that all may properly be interested
in his intended marriage, he dwells on the
intensity of his affection only to the lady
herself. These are matters relating to the
separate self, while manners give expression only to what all can share. Our ardent personal passions, even when entirely
justified, often need to be flattened down
before they can be fit to express. Mani-
festations of the social passions, kindness
and pity, are seldom improper. These
give a double opportunity for sympathy.
We share the feelings both of the sufferer
and the humane speaker. But the emo-
tions that terminate in ourselves, like joy

and grief, require care. On the whole, Smith thinks we may count on sympathy with our small joys and large griefs. Happiness is something delightful to share, at least until it becomes so great as to awaken envy. And though it is disagreeable to hear of petty annoyances, which a gentleman passes lightly by, serious misfortune is so much a part of the common lot that all will sympathize in hearing of it and be pleased that they have in this instance escaped. The death of a relative may not improperly put its mark on our very clothing, but it is indecent to speak of our vexations from servants and children.

Here, then, we see human society reposing on a widely distributed and systematized altruism. Mutual consideration is here the rule. The apostle states it admirably: "Look not every man on his own things, but every man also on the things of others." The separate self is allowed no place; the conjunct self is the only person recognized. Surely, any one who undertakes to examine the varieties of altruism must begin with these beautiful and little-noticed moralities.

Begin, but not end here. For while I

believe all that has thus far been said is
true, I see so much else to be true that I
devote a section of this chapter to a criticism of manners. Wherein do manners
fail to embody altruism completely? In
three respects: they are trivial, self-protective, and enfeebling. The study of these
deficiencies will show us the way to altruism of a higher kind.

The triviality of manners requires no
long demonstration. All must have felt it
and, probably enough, have been surprised
at my counting such matters deserving of
a place in a serious ethical discussion. It
is as if I had devoted a section to brushing
the hair. Many things more or less connected with the comfort of daily life we
do not talk or think much about, and such
are manners—never good until they become
instinctive. They express merely our super-
ficial relations with our fellows, our outward behavior, our acts and not our motives. The man of considerate manners
may be inwardly considerate, too; but he
may be the very reverse and have shaped
his conduct with a view to social success.
Indeed, it may truly be said that manners
become more prominent as the occasions

of human intercourse diminish in importance. Organized "society," in which manners flourish, is treated as of little consequence by the sober body of the community. This, then, is the first defect of manners when regarded as an embodiment of altruism: they are of limited range and do not necessarily involve the whole man.

But they are open to a graver objection. They are fundamentally self-protective. If my first account of them were the whole truth, society people would be the least selfish of mankind. That is not their reputation, for manners are, after all, grounded in distrust of our fellow man. I said that the chief aim of manners was to avoid offense; that is, we anticipate being offended when we meet, and take precautions against it. The need of such precautions against the turbulent ego I have shown already. Until I can be sure that people will not shock me by tasteless attire and heavy talk, that they will not unload on me what concerns only themselves, that they will not be tedious, didactic, or intrusive, in short, that they will be trained to play the social game for general enjoyment rather than individual gain, I shall keep away from company. Manners express these doubts. They preserve an interval between me and those who might press too near. Emerson says of them that they are a contrivance of the wise for keeping fools at a distance. No doubt they may also express affection and pleasure in humankind. I only assert that this is not necessarily their meaning. They may be mere social safeguards, restraints to which each of us submits in Hobbistic fashion in order to protect ourselves.

But there is one further point in our disparagement of manners. He who accepts the code, indorses, and practises it, finds himself in the long run enfeebled. Accordingly, a healthy nature is always a little restive under manners. The child rebels against being taught how to behave. He wants to behave as nature prompts. When full of glee he would laugh aloud, but is told that loud laughter in company is not proper. Is there not danger that the continual check which manners put on exuberant nature may, in the process of rubbing off social excrescences, rub off much of nature too? How large will be the "due opportunity for self-expression" in a society whose prime aim is "the avoidance of offense"? It must be remembered that checking expression checks thought. We do not develop strong interests when moving among those who stare if we mention them. In company, people may grow quick, clever, neat in repartee, compliment, and paradox, but they do not become reflective, solid in judgment, distinctive in individual taste. Such things come more readily in isolation. It is wise advice George Herbert gives:

"By all means use sometimes to be alone.
  Salute thyself. See what thy soul doth wear.
  Dare to look in thy chest, for 'tis thine own,
   And tumble up and down what thou find'st there.
    Who cannot rest till he good fellows find
    He shuts up house, turns out of doors his mind."

The fact is that in bidding us all the time to be regardful of others, manners make too sharp a division between the conjunct and the separate self; and it is disastrous to each to be set up to the exclusion of the other. In detachment the conjunct self grows empty, the separate self surly and brutish. They belong together. When either has been unduly emphasized, it is

wholesome to give the other a chance.
Society, the special field for the cultivation
of manners, would soon be sterile soil were
it not abandoned during lenten intervals
and summers in the country. After meeting a multitude of people and being obliged
to adjust ourselves to only such matters
as all can understand, what a relief it is to
be in the open fields, social conventions
dropped, responsibilities forgotten, and no
regard for others marking our words, acts,
or dress!

And now we see why all the words which
name the ingenious system of man's best
approach to man contain a tinge of evil.
Every one is a disparaging term, though
meant for praise. Politeness, courtesy,
good breeding, propriety, decency, civility
—manners is the best of the long list, for
it states with less of praise or blame the
mutual consideration expected whenever
person meets person. But it is not altogether clean. It lingers on the outside and
so suggests triviality, suspicion of our
neighbor, and the enfeebling of originality.
That these baser qualities are not inherent
in manners is true enough. A well-mannered man may have a friendly soul. But

he may have one of an opposite sort. Manners, therefore, though altruistic in form, are not necessarily altruistic in matter. They can, accordingly, be regarded as only the beginning of our inquiry. No human society, it is now evident, can be formed without recognizing the altruistic principle; but in manners that principle may be employed as naturally for an egoistic as for an altruistic purpose. What we are in search of is a situation in which a man sincerely prefers another's good to his own.

CHAPTER III

GIFTS

Such a higher stage of altruism is that which I have called Gifts. When we give, we set ourselves in a low place and some one else in a high, so intentionally putting altruism into the matter of our action and not merely into its form. A definition of giving would therefore run as follows: the diminution by ourselves of some of our possessions, pleasures, or opportunities for growth, so that another person may possess more.

Every gift, to be a real gift, must cost the giver something. When I have just received an unexpectedly large payment and am feeling particularly well off, I might easily take pleasure in handing a half-dollar to a beggar. But that is an amusement, not a gift. I have experienced no loss. For both money and beggar I cared little, but the momentary sense of munificence was agreeable. The act was one of pride rather than generosity. On the other hand, I give a friend a book I love, one that has deeply influenced my life and I hope may influence his. He has no means of obtaining a copy elsewhere. I shall miss it, no doubt. But remembering how long I have had it, and he not at all, I resolve to impoverish myself for his enrichment. The moment I hand it to him he becomes the rich man and I the poor. All ownership on my part ceases. I have cut myself off from something valuable in order to bring about a certain superiority in him. That is the essence of a gift. To make my friend large I make myself small.

It may be said, however, that such damage to the giver is unnecessary. Completer giving would be that where the receiver makes up to me my loss. But would not my act under such conditions cease to be a gift? It would become an exchange, a trade, a bargain. Whether a wise trade or a foolish, there was calculation directed to keeping me as well off at the close of the transaction as at the beginning. On that account no one will call it a gift. Or if, again, I expect positively to profit by what I offered my friend, finding my book-

shelves crowded and resolved to lead a
simpler life, my act once more will lack
the quality of a gift. Wisely I rid myself
of some superfluous possessions, but I did
so quite as much for my own advantage as
for that of my friend. It is true that often
in whole-hearted giving we find ourselves
in the end richer than before. But that
was not contemplated. What we sought
was impoverishment for another's gain,
and it is that purpose which constitutes a
gift.

As regards what is given, a few words
may be well. All gifts are not of the same
grade. In thinking of them we generally
have in mind parting with a piece of property. But this is the slenderest of gifts.
Accordingly in my definition, side by side
with possessions, I named a superior sort
of gift, pleasures. To detach a pleasure
from myself for another's sake, and to succeed in the difficult business of transferring
it from my enjoyment to his, is surely a
larger gift than parting with a piece of
property. Indeed, even in giving an article, I felt the pleasure involved in it to
be the important matter. Having been
pleased with it myself I trusted it would

bring my friend pleasure too. The article was a mere means, a subordinate part of the affair. Could I convey as much pleasure without it, the gift would gain in delicacy. Suppose then on a beautiful afternoon, when I have been bending over my work all the morning, I am offered a ride in the country. A friend is standing beside me, and to him I turn. "You take this seat. I do not care to go. You need it more than I." And knowing full well the refreshment that will be had, I persuade him to take my place. Here is a gift of a higher order than a mere piece of property. Its substance is taken more directly out of myself.

But there are gifts higher still, for we may give sections of ourselves more important than pleasure. I may allow myself to stagnate in order that my friend may grow. In filling out his nature, let him not merely use me; let his use me up. Here altruism reaches its highest point in self-sacrifice. Yet instances of it are common. In almost every home in the land something like this is going on. In many households parents are saying: "That boy shall have the opportunities which we al-

ways longed for but could not attain. He
shall go to college. A little pinching on our
part will make it possible." And so the
boy goes joyously forth into an invigorat-
ing world, provided by the narrowing life
of those at home. Such gifts are incomparable. They are gifts of life-blood.

Or do I distort this consummate altruism by calling it sacrifice? At least this
should be added, that true sacrifice never
knows itself to be sacrifice. Joyously the
parents send their boy forth and joyously
accept their own narrow routine. They do
so feeling that he to whom they are giving
their life is inseparable from themselves.
They have learned to merge their abstract
isolated self in him and to conceive themselves as living the larger conjunct life
with him in his new opportunities. How
exquisitely astonished are the men in the
parable when called on to receive reward
for their generous gifts! "Lord, when saw
we thee an hungered and fed thee, or
thirsty and gave thee drink? When saw
we thee sick or in prison and came unto
thee?" They thought they had only been
following their own desires.

Here, then, giving seems to supersede it-

self, the giver receiving quite as much as
he bestows. And some such paradox is
unavoidable so long as the thought of self
remains properly ambiguous. Our early
English moralists saw no ambiguity in it.
They understood by self the abstract,
unrelated individual. They were conse-
quently so puzzled by benevolence as often
to deny it altogether. In our age of social
consciousness the puzzle has largely disap-
peared. We see giving to be as natural as
getting, and hardly to be distinguished
from it. But it will be well before advancing to criticise the higher forms of altruism
to fix firmly in mind some classic statement of the two conceptions and once for
all to see how absurd each looks from the
point of view of the other. When our
Lord hung upon the cross the jeering soldiers cried: "He saved others; himself he
cannot save!" No, he could not; and his
inability seemed to them ridiculous, while
it was in reality his glory. His true self he
was saving, himself and all mankind, the
only self he valued.

Giving has always impressed mankind
as singularly noble. Indeed, in the judgment of many it outclasses all other ex-

cellence and is the only human action to call forth reverence. So nearly does generosity become identified with goodness that if I should ask a man whether John Smith was good to him yesterday I should be understood to ask if he gave unselfish attention to that man's affairs. Goodness in this sense, the disposition to give, will in the popular mind cover a multitude of sins. In how many stories have past ages taken pleasure where the robber hero, crafty, merciless, and generous, bestows upon the poor plunder taken from the rich. The man ready to give, whatever else his quality, seemed to our ancestors always to deserve admiration.

We have become suspicious. There is a disposition to-day to question this wholesale praise of giving and to suggest that it is not free from danger. Instead of promoting public welfare, generosity may sometimes impoverish the community. It may lead people to depend on others, instead of standing on their own feet. And what a general weakening follows! The two classes into which society always tends to fall become more sharply contrasted—the rich, amusing themselves from time to time with

officious charity, and the poor through accepting it steadily growing more helpless
and cringing. Our fathers, less studious
of society than we, did not perceive these
dangers, but only the evils of selfishness.
They accordingly eulogized giving, whatever and wherever it was. If a man asks
for your outer garment, give him your inner one also. Give without calculating results.

Against all this a reaction has set in. It
is now insisted that giving should no more
be freed from rational control than any
other impulse. It is too important a matter to be left to caprice and pursued merely
to give the giver ease. It should be scien-
tifically treated. The circumstances should
be studied under which gifts may be per-
mitted and under which withheld. We
should be clear about the proper grounds
for giving. Simply because somebody takes
pleasure in giving he must not be allowed
that pleasure where it becomes detrimental
to the community at large.

Such are the questionings of our time.
In studying this high form of altruism I
cannot pass them by. I may fairly be
asked to indicate when it will be safe to

open the hand freely and when we had better keep it somewhat closed. As I try to classify the conditions of giving, I notice that two are grounded in the nature of the receiver and two in the nature of the giver; and in that order I will take them up.

Obviously, the first condition to be considered is the receiver's assured need. When we see need and have the means to check it we naturally spring forward and give with reference to that particular need. If a man needs food, I do not offer him a theatre ticket; though if I found him worn with business and needing recreation such a gift would be appropriate. This adaptation is the important matter in all true giving. "Find out men's wants and wills, and meet them there," says an old poet. To give anything that happens to come into my mind is selfish and shows me unwilling to take trouble for another's sake; that is, I am shown to lack the very spirit of a giver. The same considerations fix the magnitude of the gift. A small amount given for a large need is often useless and exasperating; a large amount for a small need, wasteful and corrupting. Wise giving demands an obedient mind attentive to another's requirements and not head-strong in insistence on one's own way. If there is any worth in giving, to keep that giving clear of waste and make it as effective as possible becomes an urgent duty.

I have already distinguished three varieties of gift: articles of my own possession, pleasures which might be mine diverted to another, and a means of growth imparted to another at my own cost. These form successively higher stages of giving, the greatest gift of all being, in my judgment, the gift of growth. Curiously enough, Kant denounces this as immoral. Man, he urges, is a person, the only being, so far as we know, who is capable of self-development. To attempt to take away this power and substitute another's developing agency is an intrusion. A man's growth is the business of no one but himself. If another person can scatter a pleasure or two in his path, it is a worthy altruistic act. But for any one but himself to undertake his construction is presumptuous and, indeed, impossible. In building a house we use plastic material, which has no will. But a person is essentially active, self-directed, and beyond the reach of agencies other than his own. When we teachers offer to make our pupils wiser, we promise what we cannot perform. Ourselves we can make wiser. To our pupils we can only offer material for their use. We may tell them that by devoting themselves to study they will reach capacious lives. But such lives we have no power to bestow. If our suggestions are rejected, we are helpless. Such is Kant's extreme theory. But has he gone far enough? Have I any more ability to impart a pleasure? I certainly cannot pick up a pleasure and put it into another person, regardless of how it will be received. There must be co-operation. The receiver may turn it into either pleasure or pain. Kant's objection applies with nearly equal force against the giving of pleasures. In both cases we merely provide material, subject to acceptance or rejection, material which has proved useful in many previous cases. I give my friend a ticket to the theatre, bidding him enjoy himself and get the refreshment he needs. But I cannot be sure what he will get. He may be bored and wish he had stayed at home. There are great uncertainties in gifts, for their receivers are indeed persons, the least calculable of all beings. A piece of property I can convey to a person with some certainty that he has received it. But whether it will mean for him what it meant for me I cannot tell. In all the best affairs of life there is risk.

If the risks in offering opportunities of growth are somewhat greater than in the case of other forms of gift, the need is greater too, and the results, if accomplished, more considerable. Arrangements for gifts of this highest sort are often properly made on a vast scale. They include churches, colleges, schools, lecture-foundations, museums. These are all public agencies for promoting growth. The private means are surer, family life. Yet here how often parents will offer gifts of an inferior sort, things or pleasures, careless whether they meet the needs of growth. The truest benefactor is he who is willing to disappoint or pain us if by so doing he can open doors for ampler powers. Our greatest need is for enlargement. Whoever contributes to that is our most beneficent giver.

But human need is only one of the two claims to gifts grounded in the nature of the receiver. We should likewise pay at-

tention to numbers. If I have a loaf of
bread to give away, and all about me hun-
gry persons stand, I do wrong in handing
half of it to one of them for a hearty meal
and putting off the others, equally needy,
with a small slice. At the beginning I
should have studied numbers and kept a
fair distribution in mind. In these days
when every mail brings us three or four
demands for subscriptions to excellent
causes, which we would gladly aid, the
question of distribution becomes perplexing.
We wish to make our gifts go as far as
possible. If we are hardy and dutiful, we
plan according to need and number; if
weak and compliant, we meet each solicit-
ing letter with a formal subscription, just
enough to be counted, and feel ourselves
discharged from a difficult problem.

In my own experience it has been helpful
to readjust slightly the conception of number and to consider rather the scope of a
gift. Many years ago a wealthy man in
the West, who had worked his way through
Harvard University, said to me that he
knew there were many men at Harvard of
decided worth but unable to get the full
benefit of the place through lack of funds.

He asked if he might leave a sum of money with me for their benefit. I was not to disclose his name, was to expend the money as if it were my own, selecting the recipients quietly through personal acquaintance and giving account to nobody. I gladly assented and anticipated easy and delightful work in distributing bounty where need was abundant. But I soon discovered that giving money away was about as difficult as earning it. I was to make investments, with returns in human power and character—called on therefore to exercise no less pains and sagacity than if the investment were for my own benefit. I believe now that much of the money I at first gave away had been better thrown into the sea. It did little good to the one who received it, and still less to the public. I was too tender-hearted and fixed my mind too exclusively on the hardships of some particular student. Pity is dangerous stuff for a charity administrator. Gradually I learned that my true object of consideration should not be the individual student but the community. Through the student I was to give to the public. And would that student be a good transmitter?

That became my constant question. In studying how my gifts might get the widest scope, I gradually formulated the maxim to help only the strong and let the feeble sink. A merciless maxim it appears at first, and always requiring subtlety in application. But what right have I, in investing property for the public good, to ignore questions of return? A powerful lawyer, doctor, business man, poet, minister, or public-spirited citizen brings blessing to a multitude, and I am allowed to share in the shaping of that blessing. Shall I withdraw funds from such a cause and invest them in stock of slender security and low interest, where they can at best only ease the discomfort of an individual? That would be to overlook the scope of my gift. I used to tell my boys that the aid was not intended for their relief, but for the relief of society to which they must carry forth heightened powers. And this, I think, should be the method in all charitable outlay if we would give to limited means the broadest range of influence.

These, then, need and numbers or scope, are the conditions of giving so far as the receiver is concerned. By studying them

we learn how to proportion our gifts. Two
more remain, equally important, grounded
in the nature of the giver. They are his
ability and his knowledge; but the former,
like number, will oblige us to examine it
from a twofold point of view.

That we are to give only according to
our ability seems almost too obvious to
state; yet it is something we must never
lose sight of. In making this gift shall I
have enough left for that? That is our
constant question. In answering it I see
that ability is only another name for an
already accumulated wealth. If our ability to give is to be large, we must in past
time, before the demand arose, have accumulated stock, in which accumulation
we are likely to receive small approval
from anybody. Spending is showy and
interesting. It has a liberal air which all
commend. While engaged in it we shall
not lack those who will cheer us on. But
saving is repulsive and suspicious, seldom
calling out praise; yet it is an absolute essential of subsequent giving. The wealth
accumulated may be of many kinds—
money, learning, sound judgment—but it
must be gathered in the dark, before the

demand for its use becomes clear. How
humiliating, when need arises and the disposition to aid is upon us, to look into our
treasury and find it empty! A perplexed
soul turns to us for wise counsel and we
are obliged to tell him, if we are honest,
that we have never trained ourselves in
careful thought and should only mislead
him by random suggestions. Preparation
beforehand for the numberless occasions of
giving is the perpetual business of the generous mind. So, at least, thought Jesus.
"For their sakes I sanctify myself."

Other persons, I said, are little likely to
assist us here and are perhaps justly suspicious. Accumulation is likely enough to
be prompted by selfishness. When a man
withdraws from his fellows every day to his
study or store, and isolated there with his
own interests regards little besides inflow-
ing wealth, he certainly looks self-centred,
may actually be so, and should by no
means complain if misunderstood. Being
misunderstood is, after all, not unhealthy.
Without exposing ourselves to that risk
few of us can reach our full power of altruistic service. We need to train ourselves
for kindness in the long run, with some

carelessness as regards the conflicting
short.

I have been pointing out how largely our
ability to give depends on an already accumulated wealth. But into ability enters
one thing more, tact. Without a good supply of this, giving irritates and misses its
mark. But tact is a word of evil omen and
has such synonyms as slyness, adroitness.
I am supposed to adjust myself to the peculiarities of somebody in order securely
to gain what he would be little disposed to
give. I have studied the windings of his
mind and know just the side on which to
approach him. I set myself in the very
best light, play on his weaknesses, and
skilfully obtain much which in his unman-
aged moods he would never think of granting. Well, tact is often exercised in this
self-seeking fashion. But that is because
it is a great power, egoistic or altruistic. It
may be employed with either aim. A good
giver needs it no less than a selfish schemer.
How many would-be givers do we know
who come blundering up with gifts and
drop them upon us in a way which utterly
shocks and makes us unwilling to receive
them. Others have taken some trouble to

be kind, have acquainted themselves with our circumstances, have been able to out-flank our delicacies and hesitations, and so to make their gift received with the least sense of intrusion or obligation. What an exquisite fine art giving may be, and how it increases altruistic power! But it is acquired with effort and will be effective only after it has become instinctive. As in the case of wealth, the gaining of it must not be postponed to the time when it is needed. That will bring merely awkwardness and disappointment. It must be accumulated beforehand. One desiring altruistic skill should be training himself perpetually: as he walks the street, as he meets an acquaintance, as he enters a shop, as he sits at table. Every situation affords opportunity for swiftly sympathetic adjustment, for removing self-absorption and substituting for it that generous imagination without which no gift is acceptable. A well-equipped giver, putting himself imaginatively in the other man's place, perceives at once how his gift may be most easily received.

But besides ability, with its two branches of wealth and tact, there is a final condition grounded in the giver, that of knowledge. Of course, we cannot give properly unless we understand the case, and the larger our understanding the greater is our obligation to aid. These simple truths illuminate some moral perplexities. I read a while ago of a famine in China. Crops had failed and there was wide-spread suffering. Tragic tales were reported. In the next column of the paper was an account of airplane construction. I found both columns interesting. The same day a man I knew broke his leg. An awful affair! I hurried to his bedside and could think of nothing else than how I might help. Then it occurred to me how disproportioned were my sympathies. Thousands of squalid deaths on the other side of the globe made a spectacular newspaper item. A broken leg next door engrossed me and called out all my resources. We have all had the experience and, on first reflection, have called ourselves selfish brutes. But I believe that is an error. Helpful sympathy waits on knowledge and proportions itself by this rather than by objective need. The sufferings of China are known to us only abstractly and in outline, and only in outline

can our sympathies be accorded. But a
case which comes under our immediate inspection, disclosing all its significant details, is a different matter and lays upon us
a claim of giving which the other rightly
does not. Nearness counts. Knowledge
heightens obligation. I would not defend
absorption in our narrow circle. I have
just been urging the constant enlargement
of sympathetic knowledge. But we should
never ignore the fact that the unknown is
not as the known and that only in proportion as we know can we advantageously
help.

Through overlooking these necessary limitations of human sympathy the Stoics were
led to denounce patriotism. We should
honor man as man. Why, then, regard
an American sufferer more than a Chinese?
Because he is my countryman. But that
rests philanthropy on selfishness and makes
the needy person's relation to me of more
consequence than his suffering. The notion of patriotism which masquerades as a
virtue should be denounced as a vice. All
will recognize in such an argument a valuable protest against narrowness. But few
will accept the principle on which it rests.

All men are not alike. Relation to me does constitute a special moral claim. Shall I treat my mother as I would any other old lady, as the apple woman at the corner? I say no; and the ground of different treatment I do not find in selfishness but in superior knowledge. I have known my mother ever since I was born. In early years she studied my needs and now she is my special charge. I comprehend what she requires in heart, mind, and person as I can comprehend those of no other woman. It is at least uneconomical to lay aside all this equipment for service and give her only the care a stranger might receive from me. The family tie means something. The tie of country means something. I know the habits of thought, the half-conscious turns of feeling, of my own people. In understanding a person of another nation I go about so far, and then run up against a brick wall, beyond which all is blind. This measure of possible understanding is the measure of duty. Knowledge forms one of the two conditions of giving grounded in the nature of the giver.

Such are the conditions which the modern mind would set upon giving. Our fathers paid little attention to them. Giving was in their eyes the crowning virtue and they were unwilling to shut it within bounds. Wherever need appeared they urged one another to meet it with charity, pretty indifferent to considerations of knowledge, ability, or social result. The altruistic purpose was so admirable that it seemed to require no scrutiny in application. But we are not content to leave anything uncriticised and have endeavored to rationalize even giving. Not altogether with success, however. On examining closely the conditions I have assembled, certain inner conflicts will be noticed. Take, for example, the case of need; when another's need is greatest my ability is least. Ability does not accompany need, increasing with its increase, but tends either to remain stationary or to fall behind as need grows. A somewhat similar conflict is unavoidable between knowledge and numbers. I have shown that as numbers grow large they become empty ciphers. The mind cannot grasp their human and detailed significance. Regrettable as this fact is, we had better recognize it as inevitable, accepting as our particular charge those instances of need which lie sufficiently near for careful inspection and leaving the more vast and distant to be cared for by special experts, supplied with our means but not our ignorance. Much of our best charity must be exercised by deputy.

The fact that gifts cannot be entirely rationalized suggests a doubt whether they can form more than a subordinate instrument for expressing altruism. By what means can their defects be remedied? To answering such questions the next chapter will be devoted.

CHAPTER IV

DEFECTS OF GIVING

A COLLEAGUE of mine, an excellent classical scholar, received by bequest an admirable collection of Latin authors. In the writers themselves, in the choice editions, and the appropriate bindings he took extreme pleasure. When talking with him about them one day I asked what he intended to do with the books at his death. Would he have them given to another Latinist as fine as himself? Or would he have them go to some college library where any one might use them? He said the question had often puzzled him, but he had finally decided to send them to the auction-room. They were books he had so much loved that he could not bear to have them fall into unappreciative hands. If he gave them away, what warrant had he that they would be prized? If they were sold, nobody would obtain one unless he were willing to get it by some sacrifice. This was not a case where generosity could be trusted. Probably the matter could be more wisely settled by self-interest.

This instance makes evident the uncertain character of giving. However superior in altruistic fulness gifts are to manners, they are unfit, unless supplemented by some other principle, to form a practical rule of life. Let us examine them in detail and see wherein they fail to embody complete altruism. In their very nature I find them to be exceptional, irrational, and condescending; and I will briefly explain each of these points.

Giving is occasional and fragmentary. It cannot occupy a life. The great body of our time and attention must be directed upon individual interests. I rise in the morning after eight hours of sleep, go downstairs to breakfast, take my walk for the needed morning exercise, on returning look over my mail and the morning paper, turn to my studies, to my meals, to calling on a friend. It is all egoistic. No doubt during the day I am repeatedly summoned to attend to other people's affairs. Begging letters, interruptions, engagements of a public and business nature are not absent. They intervene and stand out isolated in

my egoistic day. No doubt, too, most of
my occupation with myself—in sleep, food,
exercise, study—is a necessary preparation
for social service. All I am urging is that
social service cannot stand alone. It requires a large individualistic background.
The care one gives to others is occasional,
one might even say exceptional. In order
to be able to meet it, our primary and pre-
ponderant care must be given to ourselves.
Such a thing as interest in altruistic giving,
separate from personal gain and established as an independent guiding principle,
is altogether impossible. Only at intervals
comes the generous act; in general, we are
busied with our own affairs.

On this inseparability of egoism and
altruism I received excellent instruction
many years ago out of the mouth of babes
and sucklings. A couple of little children,
a girl of four and a boy of five years old,
had just been tucked into their beds. Their
mother in the next room heard them talking. Listening to learn if they needed anything, she found them discussing one of
the vast problems for which the infant
mind seems to have a natural affinity.
They were inquiring why we were ever put

into the world. The little girl suggested
we might have been sent here to help
others. "Why no, indeed, Mabel," was
her big brother's reply. "Of course not;
for then what would others be here for?"
Pertinent reflection, putting the answer to
one-sided altruism into a nutshell! If our
own affairs are worthless, why suppose they
can be of worth to others? It is no kindness to bestow on another what has never
been found good for ourselves. A gift
should cost something. Something properly valued by us we part with for another's sake. A strong egoistic sense, then,
is a condition of altruistic action. The
latter cannot cover the whole of a life.
No man is benevolent all the time, but ex-
ceptionally, at intervals, when regard for
himself may safely be withdrawn.

A graver defect of giving is its arbitrary
character. Our reformers have been attempting to rationalize charity and certainly have devised methods by which
some of its worst evils may be lessened.
But until they stop it altogether they will
not rid it of irrational wilfulness. One
would say that in kind and degree my
gift should answer another's reasonable

claim. But it never does. A just claim
renders a gift impossible. Gifts come from
a region outside claims, outside rational
justification. They are the expression of
arbitrary will. I give because I want to,
and the other knows he has no right
beyond my inclination to what he is receiving. Were there legitimate grounds
for my pretended gift it would be merely
the payment of a debt and would afford
no such pleasure as does the over-and-
above of a gift. A clerk may have satisfaction in his salary, but his feeling on
receiving his employer's gift is something
altogether different. The gift dropped
from the sky. He had no idea it was coming. He really had done nothing to deserve it. Others might have had it equally
well, but by some fancy he had been picked
out for enrichment. It is this unexpected-
ness, this incalculability, which makes a gift
so good. Gifts at Christmas, which have
been systematized, are of a paler order.
Even in these there is usually uncertainty
enough left to keep them agreeable. Our
regular giver may decide to give elsewhere
this year, he may forget; what he will select
we cannot guess. The important part of

the gift is not its intrinsic worth but its expression of the giver's will. Gladness over the former springs from greed, over the latter from gratitude. This arbitrary will on the giver's part and the absence of claim in the receiver make a reasonable gift hard to conceive. To be a gift at all it must be capricious, undeserved, and only occasional.

But there is a feature of giving more obnoxious than either of these two, yet no less deeply rooted in giving than exceptionality and caprice. A gift has always something disparaging about it. It professes to honor, but deep in the heart of it there is disparagement, condescension at least. I declare another to be better than myself, preferring that he shall be the owner of something prized by me. Yet in reality I retain the superior position myself and make the one whom I honor my dependent. Rightly did Jesus say: "It is more blessed to give than to receive." How could it be otherwise? The giver is the wealthy man, the man of power and preference; the receiver confessedly the man of need, passive to another's will. The very attempt, then, that I make to raise him up and provide him with something acceptable from my store sets him beneath me. He lacks, I abound. At the very moment when turning to him I say: "I prefer you to myself and desire that you rather than I should possess this," I am really also saying: "But by all right it belongs to me and I part with it as its and your superior." However glad, therefore, we may be to get our wants supplied, a disagreeable taste is apt to lurk about the acceptance of a gift. A good share of humility is required of one who will be an altogether happy receiver, a contented inferior. Our age has discovered this and has grown restive over charity. It would seem that in past ages those who lacked the things that make life worth living stood with outstretched hands to receive them from their rightful owners, and that those who owned counted it a prerogative of their station thus to assist their inferiors. But this humble attitude of the needy is disappearing, together with many other traditions of aristocratic days. Our poorer classes now have too much self-respect to be at ease in such relations. Certainly the poor to-day are vastly better off than at any other period of the world's history, yet never more discontented. The new self-respect which has come with easier conditions makes them resent charity and dependence. "Give us what belongs to us," they seem to say. "We want no benevolence. If a better living should be ours, we will take it as of right but not by favor. We stand on our own feet, acknowledging inferiority to no man." This rejection of charity on grounds of self-respect is not uncommon to-day. I have met it in administering the little trust for the benefit of students of which I spoke. And though I do not altogether sympathize with it, I see in it much to honor.

Such are the possible humiliations of the receiver. But the giver is exposed to dangers hardly less. His gifts may be selfish rather than generous. Few pleasures are greater than giving. In it we feel our power and catch a sense of the creative efficiency of our will. One often gives for the sake of indulging this self-assertion, with small regard for the receiver. Then too, while a true gift costs the giver something, he who gives out of his abundance may hardly feel the loss, though feeling full well the glow of raising the helpless to prosperity. That glow is by no means reprehensible. It is one of our purest pleasures.

> "All earthly joys go less
> To the one joy of doing kindnesses."

But it should not be reckoned as generosity. Should we not, too, in estimating the altruistic worth of gifts deduct the many seeming gifts which are prompted by shame? When asked for a subscription, I cannot well refuse and continue to hold my place in public esteem. *Noblesse oblige.* One must pay for dignity. It will not do, then, to assume that giving is always an altruistic act. It may be. Yet even where it is genuinely addressed to improving the condition of some needy person, the danger is not absent of lowering the independence of that other, of making him through our will our conscious inferior, and accordingly implying disparagement in our very bounty. If in giving we always keep the better end of the transaction for ourselves and hand the poorer to another, few adjustments of social life will call for more tact.

Yet we are all of us receivers and generally manage to be such without loss of dignity. Under what circumstances may we and may we not preserve our self-respect and still take money? If a stranger passing me on the street hands me a five-dollar bill, I should feel myself disgraced if it went into my pocket. If one I did not know wrote from a distant State his enjoyment of a book of mine, enclosing a check, I should return the check. If finding a person in distress and helping him he offered me money, I should refuse it. Independence is dear to most of us and we do not care to part with it on grounds so casual. This is the condemnation of "tipping," that abominable practice introduced from countries more servile than ours. It cheapens him who gives and him who takes. I see only four occasions where the acceptance of money is compatible with manhood.

Where misery is so abject that self-help is impossible it is no disgrace to confess inferiority and lean on a supporting arm. Only we must insist that as strength returns the arm be withdrawn. Permanent invalidism is an insidious danger. The

second and best accredited ground for
taking money honorably is that of money
earned. Here I give as much as I receive.
Each of the two parties at some cost gets
what he desires and each gives with reference to another's need. No doubt there
are degrees of dignity in the work done.
If as a physician I sell intellectual power
and special knowledge, I am naturally
honored more than if as a day laborer I
sell only physical exertion. But work and
wages are in themselves honorable, so that
if ten cents is of more consequence to me
than getting my hands dirty, I am not disgraced by blacking another man's shoes.

A third case is of almost equal importance, though more complicated and more
liable to error. We may accept money in
trust, receiving it from an individual and
returning its results to the public. I have
already spoken of this in connection with
scholarship aids. Aids for advanced re-
search, whether from the government or
private foundations, are of the same nature. To be selected for such aid is a high
honor, justified, however, only by the receiver's proving himself a good transmitter.
He should regard the money as given not

to him but through him and be sure that
ultimately it reaches some mark other than
himself. This may be accomplished by returning an equal sum to the source from
which the aid came, by helping some other
person equally needy, or by dedicating to
public service powers raised by such aid
from ordinary to superior rank. Equivalence should be brought about. In some
way the one benefited should put back
what he has received. If he allows it to
stick in himself, untransmitted, he is disgraced.

I reserve to the last the completest
ground of acceptance, love. Where love
is, there is no superior or inferior, no giver
or receiver. The two make up a conjunct
self with mutual gain. Or shall we say
that he who loves delights to think of himself as inferior, prides himself on it, and
would be ashamed not to look up in glow-
ing dependence? To him, therefore, gifts
bring no disparagement, but happy gratitude. In such unabashed dependence most
of us spent our early years. And if as we
grew strong fewer gifts of money came to
us, their place was taken by loving tokens
more subtle, more pervasive, and coming

from more sources. Possibly we may say
that only love and exchange make the taking of money permissible, and that my first
and third grounds are only special cases of
these two. It has been well said that there
can be true giving only where the two
parties ideally change places: the giver so
putting himself in the receiver's place that
he feels the afforded relief a personal gain;
and the receiver sharing the pleasure which
under the circumstances the giver must
feel. There is always, however, a difference in the way we accept what comes by
exchange and what comes by love. In the
former our thought is fixed on what is received, in the latter on him who gave.

Such are the characteristics of the second
stage of altruism. I proposed to study
that great principle from three points of
view which would show the successive steps
by which, without injury to the individual,
it goes on to completeness. At the very
beginning of life, and ever after, we are
called on to pay attention to others and to
subject ourselves to restrictions for their
sake. We find ourselves related or conjunct beings, and on our frank acceptance
of these relations our power and peace de-

pend. Without the restraints of manners
life would be, as Hobbes said, "solitary,
poor, nasty, brutish, and short." But the
ever-present altruism here is imperfect because primarily dictated by the desire to
protect ourselves. The separate self and
the conjunct self are not necessarily united
in manners. The form of altruism may be
kept for protective purposes when there is
nothing of it within.

The next higher stage, however, starts
from within, the giver seeking to promote
another's welfare at the cost of his own.
But there is always uncertainty in accom-
plishing this; it extends at best only to
brief portions of life, is impossible wherever
rational claim enters, and never escapes a
suggestion of haughty disparagement. The
trouble in both of these stages is, after all,
the same. *Alter* and *ego* have been conceived as distinct, and getting has been
separated from giving. But surely this is
unnecessary. There are mutual situations
in life where each of two parties is at once
giver and receiver. The single self may be
entirely at one with the conjunct, the conjunct with the single. Only so in mutuality can altruism become complete. To ex-

plaining this curious situation I shall devote my remaining chapters. But before doing so I wish to turn back and make atonement for a certain erroneous light in which I have placed these earlier stages.

When I was analyzing manners my readers must have felt that those are not the manners with which they are familiar. They have never felt the need of barriers between friends or thought of manners as a protective agency. Nor in gifts have they come upon my perplexities. Giving and receiving have seemed to them matters usual and pleasant, and no notion of superiority or inferiority has entered their heads.

No doubt this is a more frequent experience than that just described. Yet my account is correct and important. It states the minimum of altruism which necessarily enters into manners, what they are when taken by themselves and unaffected by any higher range of our being. As soon as we become acquainted with giving, it reacts on this earlier stage and fills it with new meaning. Egoistic elements are softened. Manners are used as an opportunity for tactful giving. An atmosphere of kindness takes the place of restraint, the formal manners I have described being reserved for formal occasions. Fortunately this higher civilization is now wide-spread. Yet we can still detect what I would call the guarded manners of some persons and set them in contrast to the generous manners of others. People of guarded manners are ever mindful of their own dignity, hold themselves somewhat aloof, and make much of punctilio. Those of generous manners are ready to spend themselves freely for the pleasure of those about them and seem able to save any occasion from dulness with their stores of information, wit, song, and lively anecdote. These persons look after those less accustomed to society and unobtrusively help them on. But even their admirable work is exceeded by those accustomed to mutuality. These give us no impression of wealthy persons imparting to us their stores. Their work is quieter. Their manners might be called friendly. They set every one at ease and do not so much give as share, appearing as much interested in our affairs as we could be in theirs. In their presence we are simpler, cleverer, and less

provincial than we had believed ourselves
to be.

In a similar way, under the influence of
mutuality gifts become transformed. Condescension disappears. The favor is on
both sides. A giver has enjoyed something so much that he wants his pleasure
shared. Will we take part with him?
There is no stooping, no handing down to
one below. The two parties are on a level,
joined in a mutual act. "Will you do me
the favor to accept this?" is both the language and the feeling of the giver.

Matters of every-day life, so familiar that
we seldom reflect on them, I have attempted
in the preceding chapters to analyze with
something like scientific precision. By so
doing I have turned them into almost un-
recognizable abstractions. In closing, I
should like to restore them to their rightful color, and I have searched for a passage
which might present the approach of man
to man just as we daily see it, with an intimate blending of all three varieties of
altruism—pure manners, giving, and mutuality. In a passage from the Eighth
Discourse of Cardinal Newman's *Idea of
a University* I find what I want, expressed

in language of extraordinary refinement
and accuracy. It will be noticed what
prominence he gives to the negative function of manners, how in depicting generosity he sees the danger of condescension,
and how he finds the crowning excellence of
manners in that self-forgetting mutuality
which sets all at their ease.

"The true gentleman carefully avoids
whatever may cause a jar or a jolt in the
minds of those with whom he is cast: all
clashing of opinion, or collision of feeling,
all restraint or suspicion or gloom or re-
sentment; his great concern being to make
every one at their ease and at home. He
has his eyes on all his company: he is
tender toward the bashful, gentle toward
the distant, and merciful toward the absurd. He can recollect to whom he is
speaking. He guards against unseason-
able allusions or topics which may irritate.
He is seldom prominent in conversation
and never wearisome. He makes light of
favors while he does them and seems to be
receiving when he is conferring. He never
speaks of himself except when compelled,
never defends himself by a mere retort;
he has no ears for slander or gossip, is

scrupulous in imputing motives to those who interfere with him, and interprets everything for the best. He is never mean or little in his disputes, never takes unfair advantage, never mistakes personalities or sharp sayings for arguments, or insinuates evil which he dare not say out. From a long-sighted prudence he observes the maxim of the ancient sage, that we should ever conduct ourselves toward our enemy as if he were one day to be our friend. He has too much sense to be affronted at insults, he is too well employed to remember injuries, and too indolent to bear malice. He is patient, forbearing, and resigned on philosophical principles: he submits to pain because it is inevitable, to bereavement because it is irreparable, and to death because it is destiny. If he engage in controversy of any kind, his disciplined intellect preserves him from the blundering discourtesy of better perhaps, but less educated, minds who, like blunt weapons, tear and hack instead of cutting clean, who mistake the point in argument, waste their strength on trifles, misconceive the adversary, and leave the question more involved than they found it."

CHAPTER V

MUTUALITY

WE have now clearly before us the two imperfect varieties of altruism. While both recognize and honor man's relation to man, from neither is regard for the separate self excluded. Each may as well be prompted by an egoistic aim as by an altruistic. For though in manners we minutely consider how we may save another from annoyance it is always with the understanding that we are thus ourselves protected. Nor does giving escape a similar self-regard. We cannot make a gift without implying that the receiver has no right to it, without bringing him into dependence, therefore, on our will as his superior. Giving, too, can only intermittently take the place of attention to our own good. It would exhaust itself otherwise. Jesus is reported to have spent thirty years in acquisition, less than three in benefaction. Indeed, unless we heartily valued our own possessions, pleasures, and growth we could

never count them fit to constitute gifts.
It is not strange, then, that to the natural
childlike mind manners are unwelcome
and that to the disciplined reflective mind
gifts are obnoxious. It is true that these
disagreeable features are softened as higher
altruistic stages throw back an influence
over the lower; the mind disposed to give,
for example, transforming guarded manners
into generous, or even if trained in mutuality, making them friendly and cordial. In
a similar manner, where the conjunct self
has taken the place of the separate the
proud giver is superseded by the delicate
giver. But these facts only make plain
the incompleteness of manners and giving
when taken by themselves, and demon-
strate that altruism to be really known
must be studied in that highest stage to
which I have given the name of mutuality.
To this intricate and important study I
now turn.

Giving fails to reach the altruism it seeks
because its generosity is confined to one of
the two parties engaged, while to the other
is assigned the inferior position of egoistic
receiver. But is this necessary? May we
not conceive of a gift without this blemish,

a giving in which each side gives to the other, thus joining giving and getting, and abolishing all inferiority? To show how this may be I am obliged to enter into more detail than in explaining simpler moral situations. I will, accordingly, offer a general definition of mutuality and then take up the successively completer forms in which it is realized.

By mutuality, then, I mean the recognition of another and myself as inseparable elements of one another, each being essential to the welfare of each. This duality of giving has always been recognized as ennobling. Even Jesus did not seek simply to give, but to induce in those to whom he gave a similar disposition. Rightly is it counted higher than simple giving, including, as it does, all which that contains and more.

Such mutuality is most familiar to us in certain cases which for convenience I group together under the name of partnership. In a partnership a specific field is marked out within which persons agree to consider certain of their interests common. When Brown and I form a firm for the sale of shoes it is understood that thenceforth

he and I have no separate interest so far
as shoes are concerned. The stock in the
store does not belong to him or to me; and
if some one seeing money in the drawer
should ask whose it was, I should have to
answer, "It is not mine," and Brown
would similarly disown it. It would be
ours. All his would be mine and mine his.
Usual thought and speech would require
considerable readjustment to fit a condition so new. "I" and "he" would pass
largely out of use as no longer of practical
significance, "we" taking the place of
these separate symbols. "Together" would
acquire a more intimate and compulsive
meaning. Accordingly, if on some bright
morning I were inclined to go shooting instead of appearing at the office at my usual hour, I should know I had no right to
the sport without Brown's concurrence,
my time being no longer mine. Mutuality
would everywhere supersede private control. All this is familiar enough. Nobody
finds it hard to comprehend. But when the
moralist urges that higher life is possible
only as the separate self becomes merged
in a conjunct, it sounds mysterious and
seems little likely to occur.

But the partnership principle is wider than the business firm. In some degree it enters into every bargain. Buyer and seller establish a kind of mutuality. Suppose a customer on coming to my store and putting down his five dollars for a pair of shoes should suddenly bethink himself and say: "I wonder if you are not cheating me. That pair of shoes cost you not more than four dollars and seventy-five cents. By your price you are taking twenty-five cents more from my pocket than you are delivering to me." Might I not answer: "It seems to me it is you who are cheating me. You need those shoes more than you need five dollars. You would give five dollars and a quarter rather than go without them. Are you not, then, returning to my pocket twenty-five cents less than you are receiving?" In reality neither of us has cheated. We have merely made a legitimate profit from one another. Such mutual profit is involved in all good bargaining. It yields a double gain. I gain from my customer and he from me, and both are left in better condition than before. If he had not cared more for the shoes than for five dollars he would not

have come to my store. If I had not
counted five dollars of greater worth to
me than the shoes I should not have
parted with them. A curious situation
this, where two persons draw advantage
from one another! But every sound commercial transaction proceeds on this assumption. In all honest trade there is a
gainful partnership.

In my last chapter, after discussing gifts,
charity, and the generous soul, I promised
to turn to a moral situation higher still,
one of purer altruism. Are we then keeping to the order proposed? Can we suppose that a commercial transaction is of
a higher order than an act of charity? I
believe we can. As we look over the history of civilization we certainly find gifts
understood long before trade. The savage
is a not ungenerous person. When he
takes a fancy to any one he gives pretty
freely, not, of course, through any claim
or duty but merely in deference to his
native feeling. What he cannot conceive
is the double gift, a transaction in which
each is a gainer. He is ready enough to
strip himself of advantage in behalf of one
whom he likes and is pleased when he, too,

receives a gift; but that one and the same
act can yield a mutual gain he apprehends
slowly and rudely. Yet on just this condition of mutuality all honest trade is
based. It is true I must add the adjective
"honest." One can deceive under the
forms of trade as readily as under any
other forms. They shelter deception well.
In dealing with a customer I may have
some special information about the quality
of an article which he does not possess.
He is therefore at a disadvantage. No one
would maintain that all the operations of
commerce are of a higher moral order than
charity; but it may be said that every
honest mercantile transaction shows altruism of a more thoroughgoing kind than a
gift does.

This may be made plainer by a contrasted vice. Living long among college
students and observing their natural pleasure in all sorts of moral experimentation, I
have come to believe gambling the vice
most likely to wreck character. All forms
of vice are bad enough. It is shocking to
see a young man drunk. But drunkenness
grows steadily rarer, and, after all, a drinker
remains pretty much himself when the fit

is off. I have had friends of this sort who
when not in liquor showed the same interest in worthy things as other men. But
when I see the gambling habit getting hold
of a young man I despair of him. For
several reasons it is unlikely he will be
good for much thereafter. Seldom does a
vice or virtue have only a single root. On
the one hand the gambler gives up rational
modes of guidance, ceases to calculate
clearly, lives on the unexpected, and looks
for some deliverance to drop from the
sky. A hectic anxiety takes possession of
him and disorganizes his life. But there
are results worse still. Gambling, in contrast with honest trade, admits only a
single gain. I can gain nothing for myself except by damaging another. I must
directly seek his harm. The tradesman
benefits himself through benefiting his customer. His business is grounded on the
double gain. He draws profit, it is true,
from another man's pocket, but he does
not, like the gambler, stop there. He puts
back into that pocket a little more than
the equivalent of what he took out. The
gambler breaks up this mutuality and lives
as a bandit by attack. Thus dehumanized

and shut up to his separate self he rots.
When trade allows the double gain to drop
out of sight, it too becomes gambling and
shows the same predatory tendencies. Honest trade is a different matter. Its mutual
profit carries altruism through a community
more wholesomely than can any arbitrary
will.

But the partnership principle runs further still. It is the cement which binds
together a multitude of groups. A ship's
crew, a regiment of an army, stands in just
this mutual relationship. They represent
the will of no one of their members, yet no
one must detach his will from the whole.
A sailor cannot withdraw to-day because he
feels like reading, a soldier because the
coming attack is likely to cost his life. Under anarchic influence something like this
was lately allowed the Russian soldier, and
the army ceased to be. It can exist only
as a conjunct affair. Our States were once
supposed to have established a Union; but
when South Carolina set up a separate will,
regardless of the rest, chaos came. How
transformed the youngster is when he goes
out with the baseball team! He does not
mind if he breaks his finger, covers himself

with dirt, or becomes utterly exhausted.
What does it matter if only the team wins?
There is no longer any *me*. He thinks in
conjunct terms. He will not shirk, take
himself away and leave the others to their
harm.

How far can such a notion of partnership
be carried? Evidently to all clubs whose
members recognize themselves as also members one of another, each forming no de-
cisions of his own. Would it apply to
churches and learned societies? Not altogether, I think. We have hitherto meant
by partnership a terminable union of specified persons for a definite time and in
reference to a definite end. In scientific
societies, and especially in churches, we do
not limit numbers and usually expect the
union to be a permanent one. This in-
definiteness as regards time and persons is
no accident. It rightly belongs to unions
like these, which aim at developing personality. A baseball team, a ship's crew,
gather a specially trained company for a
particular end. When this end is attained
the union naturally ceases. Science and
righteousness are never attained, but appeal without limitation. Perhaps, then,

such internal and personal associations should not be classed as partnerships at all, but that notion should be reserved for unions of a more external and limited sort.

If I am right in this, it may help to explain the hesitation many readers must have felt over my eulogy of business methods as examples of altruism. Certainly we all know that commerce has a barbarous side. Nowhere else among civilized human beings does selfishness become so ruthless. The possibility of this comes through two limitations which partnership sets on mutuality. When Brown and I established our firm we limited the persons involved to himself and me, and even we were to have relations only so far as concerned the sale of shoes. Within these two limits mutuality was complete, but it did not extend beyond. Supported thus by one another, we two were able to contend with the rest of the world as neither could alone. Together we could push our interests with little regard to the general interests of the town. If other trades suffered, we need not care so long as the shoe business flourished, and still less need we care if our prosperity crowded out of existence the

shoe store on the opposite side of the street.
Such clear limitation of an altruistic horizon
is always dangerous. In many restricted
unions the danger is noticeable. A family
warmly considerate of its own members
often shows small sympathy for persons
beyond its bounds. A ball club, a secret
society will practise trickeries on other
leagues which their members as individuals
would scorn. In trade, too, the matter is
made worse by a second limitation. My
partner and I understand that our mutuality operates only with reference to the sale
of shoes. We do not merge our lives. We
keep a sharp line drawn between them and
our business. Possibly enough I may have
little respect for Brown. As a person I
may think so meanly of him that when he
suggests being asked to my house and
meeting my wife and children I find an
excuse for not inviting him. He is excellent so far as selling shoes is concerned, but
personal relations are quite another thing.
Here again the narrowing of the field within which mutuality operates lessens its dignity and intensifies its aggressive power.

No wonder, then, we are apt to picture
trade as a conscienceless struggle of com-

petitors for private gain. But the picture is disproportionate and erroneous. Savagery is possible here, but so is much else. Commerce has a deep ethical ground and wide ethical opportunities, co-operation being as essential to it as competition. It exists only through service to the community. The mutual relations of partnership are constantly being extended, single trades organizing to promote their common interests, and chambers of commerce overseeing the business of a whole city. Those who engage in trade are no less human beings than their fellows and are continually discovering that honorable and high-minded methods of conducting business are in the long run profitable. The very competitions that arise are useful promoters of efficiency, and the general government stands ready in the background to fix limits beyond which greed shall not go. There are, in short, many circumstances in the life of trade which to a good degree neutralize the limitations which I have pointed out in its application of the principle of mutuality.

That principle, too, runs far beyond the field of partnership. Partnership brings persons into mutual relations only with reference to certain external ends. Brown and I joined only those fragments of our lives which were connected with the sale of shoes. We might join extensive portions, might merge not merely our occupations but all our personal interests. In him I might discover what contributes to my best growth and he find no less in me. In this way we should reach a new species of existence to which the definition of mutuality previously given would apply in a higher sense. I should here recognize another and myself as more completely constituent members of one another, each being essential to the welfare of each. Here no new elements enter which were not included in partnership. There as here identification of interests appears, the abolition of mine and thine, the double gain; only here there is no restriction of the field. The lives are identified throughout their full depth and extent. They do not merely collaborate for a specific purpose.

Such is the attitude of love, so familiar, so mysterious, so potent in developing whatever is best in us. In it both egoism and altruism have ample room. If I loved

Brown, I should not hesitate to own that I
sought him for my own advantage, though
I should also bid him to take of me all
he wanted—the more, the better. And I
should expect the same double response
from him. Edmund Spenser has stated the
matter with great precision in his "Hymn
in Honor of Beauty":

"For love is a celestial harmony
  Of likely hearts composed of stars' consent,
  Which join together in sweet sympathy
  To work each other's joy and true content,
  Which they have harboured since their first de-
     scent
  Out of their heavenly bowers, where they did see
  And know each other here beloved to be."

Spenser intends by "harmony" what I
have meant by mutuality, something where
several different parts belong together and
reach their full significance in union. If the
two hearts are similar and each merely re-
peats what the other contains, there is no
mutual profit. They must fit one another,
and in this fitting there is always something of the unknown. They cannot of
themselves entirely create the union. The
"stars' consent" must be added. Heaven

must shine upon them. Spenser even suggests that their adaptation to one another is not begun in this world, but is merely recognized here as having been ever of old. Once known it brings them full content.

This, then, is the topic to which we now turn. It is that which the ethical teachers of every age have counted fundamental. With Jesus it supersedes all else. Writers as unlike as the Catholic statesman Augustine, the Jew Spinoza, the Puritan Jonathan Edwards see in love the fulfilment of righteousness. "Love God and do as you please," says Augustine. It is something we all experience and few understand. In it there are paradoxes not found elsewhere. Delicate analysis will be needed to bring out all that it involves, to show, too, how even here limitations creep in. To this puzzling and attractive work I devote the next chapter.

CHAPTER VI

LOVE

In the *Symposium of Plato* Socrates is made to say that he can profess knowledge of only a single subject, love, but that through acquaintance with this he has a key to unlock all wisdom. And certainly if Socrates understood love he deserves to be reckoned among the wise. Few have looked into it soberly. To those who are not experiencing it, it is a jest; to those who are, a blind passion. Novelists exploit it for cash; poets, on the whole its most serious students, too often for graceful fancies. Saint Paul's compact sentences give more of its substance than can be had in the same compass elsewhere. In undertaking an analysis of it I believe I can best fix attention on its more important ethical features if I ask a series of simple questions about it and then develop their complicated answers.

(1) How does love differ from liking? Quantitatively. The degree of emotion ex-

pressed by love is out of all proportion to
that of liking. I love my friends and like
their surroundings; I like this gift and
love the giver. An exchange of terms in
either of these sentences would make moral
nonsense. Liking touches only the sur-
face; I like strawberries. Loving goes all
through; I love my old servant. Of course,
then, loving includes liking, though liking
may or may not be accompanied by loving;
and equally, of course, loose talkers, who
do not know what they mean, will try to
be impressive by using the weightier word.
I love automobiling, I love the opera, I love
ice-cream; these are all forms of silly exag-
geration which no one will seriously defend.

But there is a reason for this quantitative difference. An additional factor enters
into love and greatly increases its depth.
Love always implies the possibility of the
loved one's knowledge and his capacity for
response. It is applicable therefore primarily to persons and the higher animals,
and only in a metaphoric way suits things.
No doubt the response often fails, but it
is always desired and sought. Love seeks
to establish a personal tie. No one ever
loved without wishing to be loved.

Furthermore, between love and liking there is a sharp contrast of mental attitude. In liking, my thoughts are on myself; in loving, on another. I like whatever brings me pleasure or profit. But Browning rightly asks: "How can one love but what he yearns to help?" That is, what we love always seems to us to have such worth as calls on us for protection and the offering up of ourselves. To the lover it appears august, superior, and supplemental to anything possessed by himself. It fills him with awe and a spirit of sacrifice. Spenser addresses his lady as "My dear dread." There is nothing of this in liking. Our thoughts are there fixed on ourselves, heedless of the condition of whatever furnishes us profit. Oxen we like, because they supply our tables and till our fields. What matter if in doing so they perish? We tend the dog we love and do not let him be harmed in our service. In short, loving is our forthgoing toward one possessing a worth preferred above our own; liking, our feeling toward anything from which we derive benefit, even though inferior in general worth to ourselves.

On account of this difference love can-

not be confined to persons. Seeing a little
girl tending her rose-bush and asking her
if she likes it, I shall probably receive the
indignant reply: "No, I love it." She
means: "I think as much about giving to
it as of getting from it." It would be improper to ask a painter, a scholar, if he likes
his work. If he follows it for gain he is
untrue to it; he can really succeed only
when he loves it, *i. e.*, gives himself heartily
to it. In many cases, therefore, where
profit is abundant, it would be a kind of
impiety to speak of liking. I like my
mother, I like God. Certainly! None
gives ampler ground for liking. But for
that very reason my mind should be set
on the appropriate outgo in return. However much the patriot may like his country, *i. e.*, recognize the opportunities it affords for life, he loves it more. Perhaps
in all these cases where impersonal beings
are loved we inwardly attribute personality to them and feel that we receive from
them as much love as we give.

For that is an essential in love: it con-
templates mutuality. The loved one looks
up to the lover as truly as the lover does
to the loved. Each counts himself inferior
and only through the other capable of pos-

sessing worth. "She is my essence and I
leave to be, if I be not through her fair
influence," says Shakespeare's Valentine;
and had love reached its completion, Sylvia
would have expressed no less. This double
action is characteristic of love, while liking
has only a single end. If we will speak ac-
curately, then, we shall acknowledge that
the real object loved is neither member of
the pair but just this mutuality, the "to-
getherness," which blots out regard for any
separate self and fills each with passion for
the conjunct. "To the desire and pursuit
of the whole the name of love is given,"
says Plato in the *Symposium*. In his
"Clasping of Hands" George Herbert
charmingly develops the puzzling reciproc-
ity of love when he tries to comprehend
his relation to God:

> "Lord, thou art mine, and I am thine
>   If mine I am; and thine much more
> Than I or ought or can be mine.
>   Yet to be thine doth me restore,
> So that again I now am mine,
>   And with advantage mine the more,
> Since this being mine brings with it thine,
>   And thou with me dost thee restore.
> If I without thee would be mine,
> I neither should be mine nor thine.

Lord, I am thine, and thou art mine;
　So mine thou art that something more
I may presume thee mine than thine.
　For thou didst suffer to restore
Not thee, but me, and to be mine,
　And with advantage mine the more;
Since thou in death wast none of thine,
　Yet then as mine didst me restore.
Oh be mine still!　Still make me thine!
Or rather make no thine and mine!"

Of course such a poem can have only two stanzas, and these must closely parallel each other in every part. The resulting definition of love, making it the completed form of mutuality, would run as follows: love is the joint service of a common life.

(2) Is the lover, then, an unselfish person and does altruism, here reaching its highest pitch, exclude all egoistic regard? On the contrary, it includes and magnifies it. I have said that love always involves liking, the knowledge that an object has brought me gain and is capable of bringing more. In his loved one the lover knows a source of incomparable joy. Were his lady once his, it would matter little what else might happen. Never before has he conceived a good so great, and he knows that

hardships shared with her would be better
than the most favorable fortune alone. He
is therefore an eager seeker. Such a passion to possess is seen in no one else. Yet
the opposite may be said with equal truth.
He has lost all selfishness. No one is so
generous as he, so ready for self-sacrifice.
To please and benefit the loved one is all
his care. Let what he gives have cost him
little, and he is dissatisfied. He longs to
suffer for her sake. These are not marks of
self-seeking. But they do indicate that
the lover has reached a new conception of
self, for which he is even more ardent than
ever he was for the old. That old separate
self he now despises, and knows that only
as he loses it in the loved one will he have
any worth. Until he has thoroughly cut
himself off from his own detached interests
he will be unworthy of her. A scrap of
Persian verse, translated by Bronson Al-
cott, states the matter well: "One knocked
at the beloved's door, and a voice asked
from within, 'Who is there?' And he an-
swered, 'It is I.' Then the voice said,
'This room will not hold me and thee';
and the door was not opened. Then went
the lover into the desert, and fasted and

prayed in solitude. And after a year he returned and knocked again at the door. And again the voice asked, 'Who is there?' And he said, 'It is thyself.' And the door was opened to him." In the mutuality of love egoism and altruism are reconciled. Each of the lovers acquires a new apprehension of self, which conjunct being bears in the mind of each the name of the beloved.

(3) Is the lover in his own estimate rich or poor? Incredibly rich in what he has received, but in comparison with his lady how poor! She is immeasurably his superior. How she stooped so low is his daily wonder. But his own inferiority does not disturb him. "Love envieth not. Is not easily puffed up." On the contrary, he rejoices in emptying himself and seeing how all that is worth while in him proceeds from her. Yet the lover is a paradoxical fellow, full of contradictions and scorning consistency. He prizes himself as he never did before and daily takes on a new importance. Never till he loved was he so watchful of his looks, speech, clothes, manners. What he brings to her must be of the finest, and he is pleased to discover

in himself excellences hitherto unsuspected
which she may well accept. Tennyson well
paints the aspiring lover in "Maud":

"So dark a mind within me dwells,
  And I make myself such evil cheer
That if I be dear to some one else
Then some one else may have much to fear.
But if I be dear to some one else,
Then I should be to myself more dear.
Shall I not care for all that I think,
Yea, even for wretched meat and drink,
If I be dear, if I be dear, to some one else?"

(4) When once established, is love permanent? Certainly not. Being a personal affair it has no routine fixity, but
must continually be created afresh. Effort
is in it, intention, readiness to put aside
temporary fancies and to practise a loyal
patience. It is true that in the wise these
practices themselves become habitual and
love therefore a matter of happy course.
No action is excellent which ceases when
not consciously pressed. From the quiet
of assured love old lovers look back on the
anxious fervors of early days and acknowledge them meagre and immature. Yet
still within call they keep the resolute will

and guard against decay. For just as my
readers find it difficult to hold the thought
of the conjunct self steadily in mind and
are obliged to resist its tendency to disin-
tegrate into separate selves, so do lovers
also. By degrees the sense of mutuality
may decline, independent interests arise,
and then one of the lower altruistic forms
may take the place of this its highest. A
pair may feel themselves drawing apart
and, finding less and less in common, may
gradually content themselves with a kind of
partnership in place of love. Or one, disturbed over the breach of affection, may
seek to repair it by acts of generosity. He
may be liberal in granting his company,
his friendly cheer, to the slightly distant
loved one. But that, too, is a slipping
down. The two are then no longer in
equality. Perfect love knows no giving.
What is there to give? All mine is thine,
all thine is mine. Together we share, not
give. But as we detach ourselves little by
little, the old separate self comes back and
we hand something across the chasm. How
sad when exuberant love thus declines into
intentional giving, altering "because it
alteration finds and bending with the re-

mover to remove"! But sadder still is it
when to formerly abundant love the guarded
altruism of manners succeeds and each is
satisfied to treat the other with watchful
politeness. This is the last stopping-place
before confessed bankruptcy.

(5) But is not love always open to repair through duty? Being the highest
embodiment of morality it would naturally
seem peculiarly alive to duty. But the
very opposite is the case. It has, in fact, a
strange aversion to duty. Any suspicion
that we are expected to love a certain person alienates us from him. We cannot
force ourselves to love even when we see
it to be desirable; nor can we expel love
when we find it unreturned or unworthy.
Love insists on freedom, a certain absence
of constraint, either from a person, from
circumstance, from collateral advantages, or
even from our own volition. Like giving,
it recognizes no claim. "Love is a present
to a mighty king," says Herbert. It cannot be bought or sold. But though so little submissive to obligation, it is highly
sensitive to suggestion and unclamorous
appeal. Indeed, it soon perishes when
fresh suggestion is withheld. Indirectly,

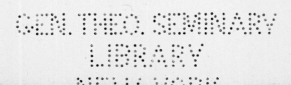

therefore, and accepting time for an ally, we can control love. I have repeatedly spoken of intention, rational guidance, resourceful care, as necessities if we would have a wise and lasting love. Those who complain of its decay have generally themselves to blame. They have imagined it constituted once for all and, while they would be glad to have it continue, have taken little pains for that fresh renewal on which its life is staked. "Keep on courting," said a sagacious mother to a young bridegroom on his wedding-day. And what has here been said of marital love applies also, with adaptations, to the love of God and the love of our fellow men. Nowhere will love submit to the direct command of duty. But indirectly, gradually, through suggestion and considerate modes of approach, it is well within our control. The Golden Rule, bidding us love God and our neighbor, is not a psychological blunder.

(6) How does friendship differ from love? Like love, it differs from partnership through having an entirely personal basis. Within its limits partnership is as genuinely mutual as love itself, but its mutuality refers to ends outside the per-

sonal lives. These remain detached and individual, merely co-operating for a time to accomplish an external purpose. In both love and friendship the personalities merge. Their interests become identified, so that one of the parties without the other is but a fragmentary being.

But friendship differs from love in the degree of intensity of its emotion and in the extent of the tract of life covered. In these respects it more nearly resembles liking. We all know how slight a friendly feeling may be, even when entirely genuine. This is because of the well-recognized limits of friendship, limits sometimes narrow, sometimes broad. I take John for my friend on account of his wit, James for his scholarship, Henry for discussion of art, Charles for theology. Outside these matters we have little in common. If I try to introduce these friends to other sides of me, I know that our friendship would be strained. Love knows no such limits. In it there is no holding back. There the more we give the more we have. Not that in friendship we set up such limits by our own volition, as is done in partnership. The limits are ingrained in the persons,

and beyond them we know it is futile to
press. When two natures have certain
sides that fit, to the advantage of each, a
friendship springs up. But how embarrass-
ing when some friend whom we greatly
value has limitations which oblige us to
pause and he, not perceiving them, at-
tributes to our adverse will the failure in
full mutual accord! Because of its narrow
bounds and because it is sought for individual gain, friendship is of far wider
currency than love. We make and drop
our friendships with comparative ease,
hardly from the first expecting them to be
lasting. But a love to which we contemplated an end, either in extent or duration,
would be already ended. The Greeks
justly eulogized friendship as our best security in an uncertain world. And, obviously, he is imprudent who does not sur-
round himself with a protecting band of
friends.

Let me, in closing this section, call attention to these varieties of personal contact, all of which are desirable. We all
need a multitude of acquaintances, can,
indeed, hardly have too many. These are
persons whose faces and names we know,

with something of their occupations and history. While we know them only on the outside our impressions of them are favorable, and their nod, smile, or passing greeting brightens the moment and makes us feel at one with our species. These do not attain the rank of friends, to whom we expose sections of our lives, in whose characters we see admirable traits which are less developed in ourselves, and on whom we lean in times of doubt, trouble, and ignorance. Such steadying friends will not be a large company and should be chosen deliberately, not through juxtaposition, but on grounds of merit and adaptation to our needs. Closer than these, however, should come our intimates, one or two, those to whom we give whole-hearted love. From such an intimate we hide nothing, not even our faults. To him we express our half-thoughts, make up our minds in company with his, find excellence easy in his presence and yet, to our daily astonishment, see that he obtains as much from us as we from him. Him we love. He is another self, and all that is ours is his also.

Such, then, is love and such its varieties and shadings. Parted from mutuality, al-

truism has little worth. Only where love
is, where the conjunct self has taken the
place of the separate self, is altruism completely realized. In such love morality attains its goal. Accordingly, in every age
those most impassioned for the formation
of character have exalted love as its central principle. The first to perceive its
importance and to begin an exploitation of
its labyrinths was Plato. To love he has
dedicated three of his Dialogues. In the
first of them, the delightful little piece
called *Lysis,* he busies himself with the
contradictions of love. He does not seek
to establish a positive doctrine. No con-
clusion is reached, but the enigmatic character of love is brought out with extraordinary vividness. The greatest of his love
dialogues, and one which has profoundly
influenced all subsequent ages, is the *Symposium,* beautifully translated by the poet
Shelley under the name of *The Banquet.*
Socrates and his friends assembling one
evening, it is proposed that instead of
general conversation they shall talk on
some specific subject, and love is selected.
One speaker after another reports what he
has seen in love—its dignity, its heavenly

and earthly types, its universality as an underlying principle of physical nature, the supposed origin of the separate self and its subsequent desire for completion, love as the organizer of human life. Then Socrates points out how the true significance of love lies in its passion for perfection and how it continually supersedes its lower forms in the interest of what is larger. The most obscuring of these lower forms, the least regardful of anything beyond itself, is that instinctive passion between the sexes which tries to monopolize the name of love. Friendship is more intelligent. Unities of a still wider and firmer kind are disclosed in the social, artistic, and scientific impulses. These are all prompted by love and follow increasing grades of beauty. Religion, however, alone reveals the full significance of these struggles toward conjunction; for God is the only complete wholeness, and every endeavor to unite with other things or persons is but a blind seeking after him. Love appears once more in the *Phædrus*, where its deeper implications are traced in connection with rhetoric and general philosophy.

At the time of the Renaissance Mar-

cilius Ficinus translated the *Symposium of
Plato* and carried its influence into all the
literatures of western Europe. Edmund
Spenser reflects that influence in his two
superb hymns in *Honor of Love* and in
Honor of Beauty. A vivacious modern
statement of the ancient doctrine is that
of R. W. Emerson in his *Essay on Love;*
and an amusing disparagement of love, as
that which interferes with the comforts
and conveniences of the separate self, appears in Bacon's *Essay on Love*. It has
been well said that any one who imagines
Shakespeare's plays were written by Bacon
should read this essay and follow it with
Romeo and Juliet. Of course, all the poets
linger in the neighborhood of love and declare it to be that which makes the world
go round. One of them, the mid-Victorian
Coventry Patmore, made himself its ex-
positor and devoted his entire product to
the systematic analysis of its every phase.
Perhaps to heighten the impression of ve-
racity, he has made the verse of his early
volumes, entitled *The Angel in the House*,
approach as nearly as possible to prose,
while his later volume, *The Unknown Eros*,
treats the same matter in a series of rap-

turous odes.   Admiring them both as I do
in an age when they are both out of fashion, I take up *The Angel in the House* when
in a psychological mood I am not disturbed
by absurdity, and turn to *The Unknown
Eros* when my ear craves music and I welcome the Platonic madness.

CHAPTER VII

JUSTICE

BEFORE advancing further it may be well to survey the tangled ground already traversed; for in mutuality, the third great section of Altruism, I have not been able to employ the simple treatment which Manners and Giving received. The principle throughout is precise and uniform. Within a specified field the interests of two or more persons are to be accounted identical, so that a double gain becomes possible, altruism transforming itself into egoism and egoism into altruism. This is the common principle which shapes every form of mutuality. But the extent of the fields specified differs so widely as to give rise to forms of very unlike moral value, which deserve separate examination.

In the field of partnership, for example, it is understood that the union will not continue indefinitely and that it has been

brought about for attaining some external
end. Partnership, bargaining, voluntary
association would not come into existence
were it not for the prospect of mutual gain.
If one party alone gains, we see that some
unfairness has occurred. Yet because in
these unions mutuality is restricted to a
small group and to the accomplishment of
external purposes, they often become en-
gines for a selfishness more intense than
their separate members would approve.
A popular proverb exaggerates but little in
saying that corporations have no souls.

But such perilous restrictions are unnecessary. There can be mutuality without them. Instead of referring to an external end, unions can be formed for an
internal purpose. The very lives and as-
pirations of two persons may be joined.
That is unnecessary in business relations.
I may dislike my partner personally, yet
judge it wise to identify my commercial
interests with his. When I make a pur-
chase at a shop I do not inquire about the
character of the dealer. With that I have
no concern. His life is his, mine mine.
Our mutual relation touches only the value
of the article purchased. And something

similar is true of our voluntary associations. I join my political club in the hope
of furthering public interests; but, to tell
the truth, I am often ashamed of my as-
sociates there. We have a common aim,
but personally I will keep myself as clear
from my fellow workers as possible. Under none of the conditions which I have
called partnership do lives merge. To
these unions for definable ends a termina-
tion is sometimes set, sometimes indefinitely anticipated.

Now, in the case of love, these restrictions are done away. Accordingly the
whole principle of mutuality comes out
there with a lucidity, power, and moving
appeal which it cannot possibly have in the
briefly planned arrangements of trade. For
though love often passes away, no such
cessation is contemplated. The eternal
vows of lovers have always been a subject
of jest. No doubt limited marriages have
been proposed. But I suspect if they ever
come about, what we mean by love will be
omitted. It would strike most of us as
absurd for me to ask Mary to join me in
identifying our lives for a single year,
sharing during that time our home, our

aims, our inmost thoughts, but always intending at the end of that time to go our separate ways, unable to say "we." External relations can be formed, dropped, and resumed, the persons involved remaining unaffected. That is not true of interior relations. These fashion a new personality to which old forms of morals, even old forms of language, no longer apply. Before advancing to explain as my final topic the special modifications of mutuality which fit it for a world principle, let me sum up the whole doctrine of love in some majestic lines attributed to Shakespeare. In 1601 a curious book appeared called *Chester's Love's Martyr,* containing a poem to which Shakespeare's name was affixed. This single fact, and the unlikelihood that any one else had such compulsive power over words, are our only grounds for thinking Shakespeare wrote the piece. It is entitled "The Phœnix and the Turtle," and allegorically describes the funeral of a pair of married lovers, the man denoted by the turtle, the woman by the phœnix. I quote only the funeral chant, omitting the picturesque introduction and the solemn ending:

"Here the anthem doth commence;
Love and constancy is dead,
Phœnix and the turtle fled
In a mutual flame from thence.

So they loved as love in twain
Had the essence but in one.
Two distincts, division none,
Number there in love was slain.

Hearts remote, yet not asunder,
Distance, and no space was seen
'Twixt the turtle and his queen;
But in them it were a wonder.

So between them love did shine
That the turtle saw his right
Flaming in the phœnix' sight;
Either was the other's mine.

Property was thus appalled,
That the self was not the same.
Single nature's double name
Neither two nor one was called.

Reason, in itself confounded,
Saw division grow together.
To themselves, yet either—neither,
Simple were so well compounded

That it cried how true a twain
Seemeth this concordant one!
Love hath reason, reason none,
If what parts can so remain."

What audacity of word and precision of thought! With what accuracy the paradoxes of love are stated! "To themselves, yet either—neither." In the first stanza the sacred word "mutual" is introduced. Where else in our language is the conjunct self so completely set forth?

Yet we cannot pause even here. To make love a principle capable of universal application, it will need to be reconstituted and, while retaining its mutuality, to be stripped of sundry restrictions.

For love is ever selective. It chooses one and leaves another. It is exercised only toward definite persons, a little group, preferably two. The smaller the number the warmer the love. But what we are trying to discover is how altruism may penetrate the whole of life, organizing society and the state. That was our ambitious ideal, and love is not comprehensive enough for it. When we give ourselves up to the single person or small group fitted to receive our love, will there not be the same danger as appeared in the discussion of partnership, that the rest of the world will be shut out? A pair of lovers is notoriously unpleasing to everybody except them-

selves. In that little world of theirs they
are so engrossed with the joint service of a
common life that what happens in the
needy world beyond is hardly noticed.
Love of this sort is pretty far removed
from universal altruism.

Nor is this danger confined to the passion of man for woman. Broader types of
love show the same exclusive absorption.
Each member of a household may be devoted to the rest and find his own gain
through devotion to theirs. Here love attains a peculiarly beautiful mutuality. But
it is still circumscribed. The family becomes sufficient for itself. Other families
do not count. Love has been selective and,
fixing its ardor on certain persons, shuts
out the rest. Even the love of God and
his children may narrow itself to interest
in those only who approach him in the
same way as ourselves. Our religious sympathy may not extend beyond our sect.
Similar perils beset national love or patriotism.

No doubt in all these cases the narrower
field may provide training for the broader;
but so long as love is selective and waits
upon personal interest it will be hard

pressed by conditioning accident. Rightly does Spenser declare that for the combinations of love the stars' consent is necessary. Circumstance, juxtaposition, plays a large part at the beginning of love. The one who would interest me may not happen to come my way; and I cannot love one whom I do not know. Obtaining such knowledge, too, even in regard to one very near, is uncertain business. I see some one who calls out what is best in me and am confident that joining with her will bring about a glorious life for us both. But can I be sure? An error in estimating will ruin not me alone but her too, whom I would honor. Knowledge, an important condition of love, is hard indeed to obtain. Nor in reckoning the hindrances to love as a universal principle can we pass by the mysteries of temperament. Many a person have we known to be lovable whom we could never love. Peculiarities of inheritance, training, habit, instinctive feeling in two persons, while not diminishing their worth, may render hopeless their adaptation to one another.

Selective love, then, hampered by its need of acquaintance, nearness, and knowledge, can never become a universal principle, binding mankind together. It shows, however, what we want. Nowhere else does altruistic fervor attain such depth. But it lacks breadth and is possible only within narrow bounds. We have been seeking to extend mutuality, the double gain, the abolition of both egoism and altruism, far beyond those bounds and reach a method by which mankind as a whole might engage in the joint service of a common life. Such an ideal would preserve all characteristics of love except its limitations. But the removal of these will affect it so deeply as to oblige a new name. I call it Justice.

Let us examine a case where mutualistic conduct shows traits beyond the reach of selective love. I go to a shoemaker and ask for a pair of shoes. He hands me a pair, I pay his price, and carry them home. As I come to wear them, I find them admirably made. They give me greater comfort than I have ever had before and wear longer. The leather appears to have been selected with care, and every nail and stitch to have received attention. I return to their maker and say: "That was a remarkable pair of shoes. Did you make them specially for me? Perhaps you have known me before, have taken a fancy to me, and so have been willing to put yourself to all this trouble for my convenience. That is the way with love. It takes burdens on itself to relieve another." How astonished the dealer would be at such talk! Would he not answer: "I had no thought of you, but I made the shoes as well as I could. It is my business." "But," I continue, "if you never know to whom your shoes will go, why take such pains?" "Because I mean to be true to my job and not shirk my part in the ongoing of the world. If I do bad work somebody, I don't know who, will suffer. I mean to be a good shoe-maker." Here is professional responsibility. The man deals justly with his unknown public.

And in such professional responsibility we pass from individual love to that noble public love which I have ventured to call Justice. Love remains, but it is now universal love, love freed from selection and without those restrictions of knowledge, circumstance, and temperament on which selection is based. No doubt in individual love there is an intimacy and a wealth of feeling which this case has not. But in it selfishness is also more pronounced. Knowing John well, I am confident that in joining my life with his, and with his only, we shall both be enriched. But the shoemaker carries his blessing to the unknown and joins himself rather with the public good. He gets his gain by giving gain to those whom he has never seen. It is true that the transaction may be partly explained on the grounds already noticed. An exchange has occurred by which buyer and seller have alike profited. But something more than calculation of profit has gone into these shoes. They would have sold readily with half the care. But this man respected business standards, was something more than a trader, gave not by equivalent measure, and was more concerned over possible danger to his customers than over extra labor for himself. That is the essence of professionalism. While frankly seeking mutual gain and declining anything one-sided, it abandons all thought of exact equivalence, keeping in the foreground standards of excellence approved by its group and looking to public service.

Or is there in the professional man something still deeper than the characteristics just mentioned, something of which these are but the outgrowth? The professional man enjoys his work and would rather do it than not. Many of us, perhaps most, are driven to work by the need to live. We will do that work faithfully and not disappoint those who depend on us. But we often think of work as toil, do as little of it as possible, and find our enjoyment quite outside it. Days of freedom from that toil are eagerly anticipated. How different is the professional spirit! It took up its work originally not as a task but as a chance to gratify a personal interest. To following that interest through all its windings its heart has been given. Throughout there has been a passion for perfection, never realized, never abandoned. Each day carries accomplishment forward and discloses wider ranges into which skill might extend. Hardship, lack of gain, failure to be recognized are matters of slender consequence. The work itself is its own rich reward.

Such is professional responsibility at its best. It is responsibility to no individual,

not even so much to the general public as
to the profession chosen. Perhaps we
catch the spirit most readily among artists
and scholars, who proverbially show little
regard for financial results. But even
where regard for money is patent and
necessary, this professional spirit is often
also present.

I am ill and call a physician. He comes
to my bedside day by day, studies my case
with elaborate care, gives up large amounts
of precious time to my whims, and never
allows his moods to intrude, so that on my
recovery I cannot help saying: "What a
sympathetic person you are! I do not
see how you can hold an interest in so
many people and feel their afflictions as if
they were your own." Such a remark
would be as inadequate as if I had said:
"You have thoroughly earned your fee."
Both would be true, and both would point
to motives which might rightly influence
him. But into that complex motive would
go a third factor more influential still, if
he was a worthy physician. He cares for
the healing art. Of course he is unwilling
that I, this individual person, should suffer.
But it is not the "me" element nor the

money element which made him take his
trouble. He would have done the same
for a stranger. And this impartial attitude
is, on the whole, best. Personal sympathy
is often disturbing. Let him coolly survey
me as a case of typhus fever, and I shall
get his best service. Through me he re-
lieves suffering, obtains for himself a due
income, gains larger knowledge of disease
and skill in combating it; in short, meets
the responsibilities of an arduous and interesting profession.

One may wonder why I call this impersonal extension of love Justice. Because
justice seeks to benefit all, but all alike.
It knows no persons, or rather it knows
every one as a person and insures each his
share in the common good. All the altruism of love is here, but without love's arbitrary selection and limited interest. We
do wrong in thinking of justice as chiefly
concerned with penalties. These are incidental, inflicted on those who refuse to
find their gain in the gain of others. The
main work of justice is its equal distribution of advantage and its insistence that
each individual shall be faithful to what he
undertakes for the benefit of all. Justice

is therefore thoroughgoing love, its mutuality guarded, rationalized, stripped of personal bias, and brought near us through the avenues of our special work.

Only we must not confine the professions to the four usually reckoned: teaching, preaching, medicine, and the law. The professional spirit may vitalize work of every sort. Here is a poor man to whom few enjoyments are open, who goes out morning after morning to shovel gravel or to engage in some other labor equally uninteresting. He earns his two or three dollars a day, takes it home, and hands it to his slatternly wife. Once he was drawn to her by romantic love. With her he figured a real union, each continually happy in the sight of the other and each day bringing to both an inward joy. He did not know her. He had neither the opportunity nor the ability to study her temperament and learn whether it was adjustable to his. It proved not to be so. Children came, cares increased, she neglected herself, her home, her husband. There was no longer any warmth of affection between them. But still he goes on working for her unmurmuringly. She is a

wife and mother, he a husband and father.
To these relationships he will be faithful.
Is not his a larger love than that of the
courtship? I do not see that we can say
so. But it is love of a different sort and a
very noble sort. We called love the joint
service of a common life. Though she no
longer joins him, he joins the community
in maintaining the family tie. What keeps
him going is his professional responsibility. Being a good husband is the task assigned him in the general division of labor.
He recognizes its justice, controls his tem-
per, and patiently meets the hardship involved. I cannot see how there is less professional responsibility here than in the case
of the shoemaker or physician. Indeed,
wherever any one is true to his specific
task, puts his heart into it, works not for
money alone nor through interest in a single individual, but, without calculating any
equivalence between what he gives and receives, studies how he may most fully perform the work to which he.has been called,
that man is exhibiting professional responsibility, honoring love, and exalting
justice in a way to deserve profound reverence.

CHAPTER VIII

CONCLUSION

LOVE is so often proclaimed as a social panacea that I have thought it well to subject it to a careful criticism and indicate its defects when regarded as a complete embodiment of altruism. Some of those defects are incidental. Since it is an affair of human beings it cannot fail to show the imperfections characteristic of such wayward creatures. Seldom does even marriage, love's best opportunity, attain that full mutuality which I have eulogized. Self-assertion intrudes early. The interests of one or the other party become predominant, and mutuality gradually declines. When the simple-minded man was told that in marriage two persons become one, he naturally enough asked: "Which one?" Yet if the completely conjunct life is rare, it is precious as an ideal for directing conduct. We often speak of love as something we fall into. Rather it is something to be made, developed, steadily approximated. The best marriages are accomplished works of art, yielding large rewards through all their progressive stages. But love is ever unstable. Unwatched, it slips down among the lower forms of altruism.

These defects of love are, however, but incidental and such as are common in all man's undertakings. There is nothing in love which can render it immune from human infirmity. But there are also in it certain fundamental defects which prevent it from becoming an organizing world-principle. At least before it can weld individuals into societies and states it must undergo large transformation and appear rather as justice than domestic affection. For love is naturally selective and individual, picking out one and rejecting another. It does not offer its bounty alike to all. Private altruism, it might be called, so that it always seems indelicate to speak of it in public. It concerns only those immediately involved and only their most intimate experiences. From such limitations it needs to be freed before it can become formative over society. All that is conjunctive in it must be retained and only its exclusions removed. In this way general justice will supplement individual love. All the varieties of mutuality are alike in joining self-regard with extra-regard. They differ only in the extent of that extra-regard.

In my last chapter I began the discussion of that superpersonal love which I called Justice. It is concerned with functions rather than individuals, and love is thus extended to a multitude who still remain unknown. To keep the framework of society steady large co-operation is required, each of its members becoming responsible for the working of some one among its many functions and having his own well-being bound up with its. To that function each is to devote himself as the lover does to his lady, and through it he sends his benefactions abroad to whoever stands in need. Such is the ideal of professional responsibility; and whether seen in shoemaker, doctor, or head of a family, it is something of wider scope and more generous impulse than private love.

Yet even in professional responsibility an element of selection remains. After studying the needs of the community I pick out

what work I will do. On some single need
I fasten—the need of settling quarrels, and
I become a lawyer; the need of instruction,
and I become a teacher; the needs of the
breakfast-table, and I become a grocer. In
all these cases my service is given not to
man as man, but only to a section of men,
to those who are conscious of a certain
specific need. It is possible, however, to
extend justice and, not confining attention
to wants already known, to endeavor to
enlarge the whole intellectual horizon of
our fellows. Thus love becomes peculiarly
impersonal and creative.

For example, when I become an artist or
scientific man I do not know precisely
what I shall contribute to the good of the
public. The public itself has experienced
no want of the wares which I shall furnish.
In devoting myself to the higher mathe-
matics I am pursuing something for which
a practical application may never be found.
But that uncertainty should not hold me
back. I know that the mind of man moves
off in that direction. I will follow and see
how far it can be pressed. These investi-
gations I am making in astronomy are
curious. They satisfy my passion for know-

ing. Believing they will satisfy that passion in others also, I ask no more. Passing beyond the immediate application of my results, I simply aim at developing persons more fully as persons, so that their capacity for knowledge may be increased. Just so does the artist attempt to reveal aspects of beauty hitherto unperceived. When he furnishes what has been done before, what men have learned to enjoy and now demand, he is a professional workman and belongs in the preceding class. But a true artist explores phases of unacknowledged beauty. Having himself seen what others have not seen, he takes the risk of announcing it, certain that if it is comprehended he will open men's eyes to fresh enjoyment. Rightly therefore do we hold artists and scientific men in high honor as enlargers of humanity. We see that altruism like theirs calls for risk and special disinterestedness. They are discoverers, going out into wide lands, far from sure what will be found there, but ready to sacrifice themselves for possible human betterment. Intellectual soldiers, we may call them, accepting the risks of doubtful battle. Theirs is a lofty altruism, and none the less because success may bring them fame and fortune.

Perhaps I strain the word justice in applying it to them, yet they as truly as the professional man do not pick out individuals as receivers of their benefits. Indeed, that absence of particularity so emphasized in justice goes to such a degree with them that their work seems to proceed from the spirit of science or spirit of beauty rather than from a particular person. They strike us as transcending their age, their own peculiarities, and to embody the conjunct self of humanity.

Still another form of justice, or of love, which passes beyond the individual, is the service of institutions. Artists, scientific and professional men all follow interests of their own, believing, however, that their work in the long run will benefit the public. But in the service of institutions not only does the public receive a benefit, it fixes also what our work toward bringing it about shall be. Personal choice, therefore, altogether disappears. The action is conjunctive throughout. But to understand this dark saying we must bring clearly before our minds what an institution is. It is a large term which we are apt to allow to fill out a big gap in our knowledge.

I mean by institutions those fairly permanent relations between persons which past experience has established for the promotion of human welfare and successive generations have approved. Ever since civilization began men have been experimenting how to live together most helpfully. The results, tested by the induction of ages, become the inherited habits of individuals and the institutions of society. Maintained through passing years, criticised, readjusted to meet more fully the needs they were intended to fulfil, they furnish each of us a working capital as soon as we enter the world. We are not obliged to decide in childhood whether to have three meals a day, whether man's dress shall differ from woman's, whether to have provision made for our instruction, worship, settlement of quarrels, safety on the street. These matters were considered before we were born, and judgments about them form our most precious inheritance. It is a veritable bank stock of experience on which to draw for our support. We accept it all as a thing of course at first, then begin to scrutinize it, asking how far these particular institutions save social friction, open avenues for enlarged activity, and how far that which once served these ends serves them no more.

Such institutions are intended for the general good. By identifying ourselves with them we both share in that good and exercise an impartial love for mankind. For these have an influence over men unequalled by any other agency. They fashion us in our unconscious years and carry forward our purposes in years of discretion. To comprehend their consolidated wisdom and conform ourselves to it will be our chief means of serving our fellow men; to neglect or weaken them through individual caprice is to be an enemy of society. Only we must discriminate in our modes of strengthening. An institution is not proved good by the bare fact of its existence. Perhaps the presumption should be in its favor, for it could hardly get itself established if injurious. But its original adaptation to human wants is unstable, and strengthening it will really mean fitting it more neatly to present circumstances. To maintain its outward form when it no longer serves its purpose is to be unfaithful to it. Constructive criticism is constantly required if institutions are to be kept sweet and wholesome. Only it should be borne in mind that changes in the framework of society can best come about slowly and only at the desire of large groups of those affected. Presumptuous, indeed, is he who will attempt to stand outside any of our fundamental institutions. The setting up of his individual will against the general will proves him no true socialist. He should remember that since everybody is wiser than anybody his first business is to conform to the institutions into which he is born, then to study elaborately their meaning, and finally to persuade his fellows to join in readjusting them with a view to their more effective working. Our love for our fellow men is shown each day in our maintenance, critical study, and reform of the social institutions around us. They survive only through our constant approval, are too important to be neglected or lightly set aside, and too liable to decay to be left uncriticised.

It is obvious, however, that institutions are of many grades of importance. Some are fundamental, as the family, property, democracy; others are local and individual, as Harvard University, Boston, the Episcopal Church, the Democratic Party. As they become narrower our acceptance of them changes its character, affectionate loyalty playing a larger part, dutiful obedience less. A member of a college, for example, comes to think of it almost as a person, symbolized in Alma Mater, and gives to it the loving devotion he would feel for a revered friend. Members of institutions so individual are apt to take their membership as something like a personal trust and to pride themselves on fidelity to it. But because such institutions are of limited range and not applicable to all mankind, failure in allegiance to them is generally regarded not as a moral lapse, but as an error of judgment.

Such are some of the aspects of justice, the impartial love of our fellow men. When we are commanded to love our neighbor as ourself, we cannot excuse ourselves by saying that love does not move by command but takes its own way according to individual temperament. Even of the simpler forms of love this is only partially true; wisdom, purpose, and patience being also essentials of permanence even in our private loves. But that public love to which we are summoned is no mere emotion, arising blindly and passing with the mood. It is the rational acceptance of our place in a social organization where all are dependent on each. A good synonym for what I have called justice would be public-mindedness.

And in this extended and superpersonal love altruism attains its fullest and steadiest expression. But so does egoism, too. That abstract egoism, it is true, which seeks its own gain regardless of that of others, is submerged. It was always fictitious, and rapidly conducted him who pursued it to emptiness. But that conjunct self, the person constituted through relations, finds in this justicial love his large opportunity. In like manner the abstract and sentimental *alter*, figured as that uncriticisable idol to which individual interests must daily be offered up, is overthrown and shown to have reality only in the degree in which it fosters personal life. Socialism which does not promote individuality, individuality which does not

tend toward an ever-completer social consciousness, are alike delusive. Each must
find its justification in the service it is able
to render to its pretended foe. Pure gifts,
to individuals or the state, are rightly ob-
jects of suspicion. Only when transmuted
by mutuality can they be kept free from
taint.

Such at least is the doctrine of this
book. In it there is nothing new. Vaguely,
waveringly, and with but a half understanding, I believe it has ever guided the
best endeavors of mankind. I have only
hoped to drag it into clearer light by a
novel sort of approach. The dangers of
that mode of approach I readily see and
wish my readers also to see. As a peda-
gogue I have torn apart things which
belong together and have separately exhib-
ited our protective, generous, and identifying impulses as successively different aspects of the altruistic life. In this way we
teachers are obliged to proceed, picking to
pieces a concrete whole, even when our
aim is to show wholeness. But my readers
will not be so simple as to imagine that
things occur in experience so disjointed as
on my pages. Life is more closely com-

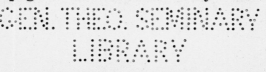

pacted than our expositions. Higher stages
and lower move forward together, assist-
ing one another. The disparagements
which I put on the lower varieties of altruism these deserve only so far as they are
detached from the higher. In conjunction,
the higher altruisms ennoble the lower and
are themselves enriched and diversified
by whatever inferior stages they absorb.
Among the ingredients of character none
can safely be thrown away. We study
ethics merely to find a place where each
may be helpful to all.